COMPLETE

Technology and Design

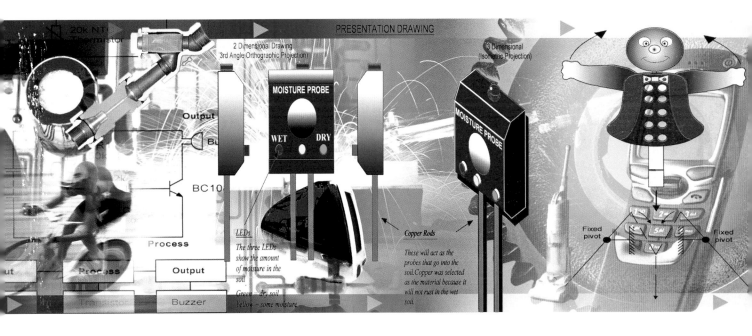

PRESENTATION DRAWING

2 Dimensional Drawing
(3rd Angle Orthographic Projection)

3 Dimensional
(Isometric Projection)

LEDs
The three LEDs show the amount of moisture in the soil.
Green – dry soil
Yellow – some moisture

Copper Rods
These will act as the probes that go into the soil. Copper was selected as the material because it will not rust in the wet soil.

Raymond Caldwell

Hodder & Stoughton
A MEMBER OF THE HODDER HEADLINE GROUP

Photo acknowledgements

The publishers would like to thank the following individuals, institutions and companies for permission to reproduce photographs in this book. Every effort has been made to trace ownership of copyright. The publishers would be happy to make arrangements with any copyright holder whom it has not been possible to contact.

Action Plus/Glyn Kirk (141); Life File/Emma Lee (3,5,6,11,57,151); Mecmesin Systems (153); Scalextric (146).

All other photographs supplied by the author.

Acknowledgements

The author is grateful to the following individuals and organisations for their support in the writing of this book:

Denis Currie, Sidney Conn and Ronnie Lee for technical editing, Glenn Currie for extracts from his GCSE portfolios, Paul Rodgers for building and testing of projects, Colum Barton without whose support this book would not have been possible, colleagues at the SELB Technology Unit for their support, Raymond Moffett for the photos of student's computer control GCSE projects, SMC Pneumatics for illustrations and technical advice. A number of the electronics circuits were developed using Crocodile Clips software. A number of the electronic PCBs were developed on PCB Wizard software.

This book was written in association with the Southern Education and Library Board.

Orders: please contact Bookpoint Ltd, 78 Milton Park, Abingdon, Oxon OX14 4TD. Telephone: (44) 01235 827720, Fax: (44) 01235 400 454. Lines are open from 9.00 – 6.00, Monday to Saturday, with a 24 hour message answering service. Email address: orders@bookpoint.co.uk

British Library Cataloguing in Publication Data
A catalogue record for this title is available from The British Library

ISBN 0 340 78244 7

First published 2001
Impression number   10 9 8 7 6 5 4 3 2 1
Year   2006 2005 2004 2003 2002 2001

Copyright © 2001 Raymond Caldwell

Cover illustration by Zap Art.

Typeset by Fakenham Photosetting Ltd.

Printed in Italy for Hodder & Stoughton Educational, a division of Hodder Headline Plc, 338 Euston Road, London NW1 3BH.

CONTENTS

CHAPTER ONE Focused Tasks Associated with Designing

Your role as a designer within technology and design is to select a situation or problem for which there is no existing solution and, using creativity and imagination, to come up with a possible answer in the form of a suitable product. However, the task does not stop there. You are then required to make and evaluate your design.

The first two chapters of the book will help you do this by setting out a number of **focused tasks** designed to develop specific skills and knowledge. Examples of students' work will be used where possible.

The focused tasks fall into two main groups:

- Designing
- Communicating

There are three main areas of designing. The following tasks in this chapter are designed to help you with these. They are:

1. Investigation of design situations
2. Product analysis
3. Product evaluation

Investigation of design situations

Investigation of design situations, or design problems as they are sometimes called, will be the starting point for most design-and-make projects you undertake in technology and design. The ideal situation is one for which there is currently no satisfactory solution. This focused task is an opportunity for you to practise and develop this skill before starting on your major design-and-make project.

It is possible to break down the focused task into five small sections. Each section should help guide you through the activity. They are:

1. Identify a small number of situations.
2. Explain each situation.
3. Select one situation for further study.
4. Research and investigate the chosen situation.
5. Write an open-ended design brief.

1 Identify a small number of situations

Identify a small number of different situations (usually three) that have the potential to lead to the design and manufacture of a technological product. There are a number of ways of finding different situations or problems. You could consider:

- your hobby or sport
- problems around the house
- existing products
- aids for the disabled
- educational aids or toys for young children
- safety within the home
- personal safety
- environmental control systems
- aids for your pet.
- It is also possible to consider a system or circuit from a theory lesson and find a situation that you could solve with this system.

2 Explain each situation

Next write a short paragraph that explains each of your situations in more detail. If possible it is a good idea to take a photograph of each of the situations and refer to this during the explanation.

3 Select one situation for further study

Select one situation from section 2 that is suitable for further investigation and write a short paragraph to explain why you have selected this one over the others.

4 Research and investigate the chosen situation

Carry out some research and investigation into your chosen situation. This is where photographs showing the problem can really help explain the situation. If possible, interview the people who are familiar with the problem and record their comments.

5 Design brief

Write a design brief for your chosen situation. A brief should be a short paragraph about what you intend to design and make. It is important to write an open-ended design brief that identifies a need or opportunity but keeps your design options open.

Investigating design situations

The following extracts are from a student's portfolio. They set out four situations that are then explained in brief. One is then selected and an investigation is carried out. Finally an open-ended brief is written.

1 Identify a small number of situations

Four were identified. These were:

1. Watering plants in the greenhouse
2. Aids for elderly relatives
3. Getting wet while open and closing the garage door
4. Comforting a crying baby

2 Explain each situation

All four situations were explained with the aid of photos. For example:

● Situation 4 Comforting a crying baby

My nine-month-old nephew wakes up very early in the mornings. His mother is frequently in the kitchen making breakfast and fails to hear him crying. The crying wakens his older brother, who is sleeping in the next room.

Figure 1.1 *Picture of the baby in his cot*

3 Select one situation for further study

All four situations were commented on and one selected for further study (Table 1.1).

The selected situation was number 4, 'Comforting a crying baby'.

Table 1.1 *Selecting a situation for further study*

Situation	Comment	Accepted/Rejected
1	I have decided not to continue with this idea as I feel the final solution may well involve plumbing and I think this may be outside my capabilities.	Rejected
2	I have given this situation much consideration but feel the solution may well involve some lifting device and due to the safety implications I have decided to stay clear of this situation.	Rejected
3	The situation, 'getting wet while opening the garage door' appeals to me and would be well worth considering but I think I like number 4 better. It has possibly more scope for a technology and design project than this one but I may come back to this one.	Rejected
4	I have chosen idea number 4 because this problem is more urgent. The thought of working with children appeals to me. Also I think the situation lends its self to designing a product for which there is currently no satisfactory solution.	Accepted

4 Research and investigate the chosen situation

As part of my investigation I have chosen to interview my aunt and uncle, who are the mother and father of the baby, and record the findings. I also plan to take photographs of the situation and make further observations of the problem.

Figure 1.2 *Picture of the baby's cot*

Student's interview with the baby's mother
The following are the notes the student made during the interview with the baby's mother

Student At what time in the morning does the child wake up?
Mother Around 6am.

Student How does this bother you?
Mother It does not bother me as much as his brother in the next room. It wakens him out of his sleep.

Student What does the child do when he wakens?
Mother Cries until he is lifted.

Student Is there anything you can do to comfort him?
Mother Yes. He responds well to nursing and he also responds well to musical toys and toys with movement.

Student's conclusion from the interview
It would appear from the interview that there is a real problem here that I might be able to help with. It would also appear that the child can be comforted by nursing, music or movement. I think that I have enough information about this situation to proceed.

5 Design brief

Design and manufacture a device that could be located close to or be part of the baby's cot. This device should have a calming effect on the child and if possible be educational.

Product Analysis

Figure 1.3 *Dyson vacuum cleaner*

Product analysis can be a useful exercise when considering an existing product that you might feel could be redesigned or improve on.

The *Dyson* vacuum cleaner is a good example of a product that resulted from product analysis. As the user of a domestic vacuum cleaner, Mr Dyson was unhappy with its performance and started to analyse it. From this simple process was born one of the most successful vacuum cleaners on the market, the *Dyson*.

While no one is expecting you to design a new cleaner, this technique can be used on more modest products and often forms the starting point for a new design.

It is possible to break this focused task down into five sections that should help guide you through the activity. They are:

1. Set out a clear description of the purpose of the technological product. Try to speculate on, and justify your understanding of what the designer had in mind when he/she conceived the product.
2. Determine the extent to which the product would meet the needs of a typical user group.
3. Discuss the method of manufacture, including the materials used.
4. Discuss how convenient the product is to use and service.
5. Analyse in general terms the input and output of energy in the operation of the system.

When undertaking a product analysis you should select a technology product you are familiar with. Keep your selection simple: unless you are a qualified automotive engineer do not try to analyse the internal combustion engine! Start with something like a pair of scissors, battery operated torch, desk lamp or hairdryer.

Case study	Product analysis of a hairdryer

If you wish to practise the skill of product analysis you might like to complete this case study. To help you with this task parts of it have been done for you.

1 Give a clear description of the product

This can be obtained from a number of sources, such as the user manual that comes with the product, catalogue books or in-store promotional leaflets.

The product selected for this case study was a 1800 watt dryer. It has a deep bowl diffuser which allows larger sections of the hair to be dried at the roots for a fuller, more natural look.

Figure 1.4 *1800 watt hairdryer*

Speculation on what the designer had in mind
The following are just a few points the designer appears to have had in mind while designing the hairdryer. You may have more that you wish to add to the list.

- Dry hair more quickly, hence the 1800 watts of output power.
- Include a deep bowl attachment to the air output nozzle. This feature is designed to add the appearance of volume to the hair.
- As the product has to be held for long periods during drying it must be made from lightweight but attractive materials.
- As the dryer is giving out 1800 watts in the form of heat the product must be made from heat resistant materials.
- Consider the product's life expectancy.
- Consider how the product will be manufactured.

2 Meeting the needs of a typical user group

Members of the family who use the hairdryer were asked how well it met their needs. These views formed the basis for a questionnaire. Other people with the same hairdryer were asked to complete this and the findings summarised. Some other friends were asked to try the hairdryer and complete the questionnaire.

You may wish to try this exercise with *your* hairdryer.

3 Analysis of the manufacture and materials

Analysis of materials
When designing a product a number of factors are important and you should comment on these during the product analysis. Analysis of materials used in the hair dryer might consider:

- heat resistance
- manufacturing processes necessary
- durability
- cost
- availability of the materials
- environmental considerations during manufacture and at the end of its useful life
- colour
- users' expectations.

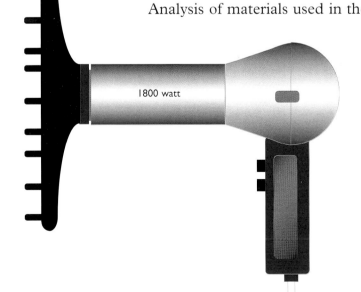

1800 watt

Figure 1.5 *Hairdryer*

Example: Heat resistance

The main body of the hairdryer would need to be made from a material that lends itself to large scale production yet can withstand the heat from both the hot air and the heating element.

Solution: A plastic such as Melamine could be used. This material can be moulded, has a high quality finish and will not change shape with heat.

Analysis of manufacture

It is important to understand how the product was manufactured. To do this you will need to refer to the appropriate sections of this or other books. Once again it is useful to make a drawing of your selected product, which you can then refer to during this section.

Manufacturing processes you might wish to consider are:

- making by wasting
- making by fabrication
- moulding
- final assembly techniques
- scale of production
- cost
- availability of components
- hazards associated with its manufacture.

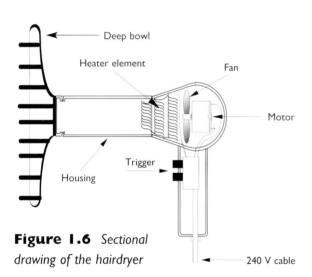

Figure 1.6 *Sectional drawing of the hairdryer*

4 Ease of service

Comment on the serviceability of the product. You may also wish to comment on safety during servicing. If it is a throwaway product you may wish to comment on the impact this might have on resources and the environment.

The bowl diffuser of the hairdryer can be removed for cleaning in hot soapy water. The hairdryer itself is a sealed unit, which is not designed for servicing. This will mean the product will have to be thrown away if it is faulty. This type of design thinking can, and often does, have a serious impact on our natural resources. Many of the components used in the product, such as melamine, decompose very slowly and will have a long-term impact on the environment through unnecessary pollution of landfill sites.

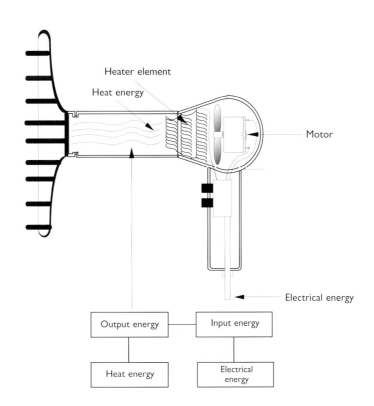

Figure 1.7 *Input–output
energy*

5 Analysis of the input and output of energy

When analysing the input and output of energy in the operation
of the product, you may wish to consider: cost of the energy,
efficiency and energy changes.

The electrical energy coming in from the mains supply goes to
the heating element. The fine wire used to make the element
starts to get hot as the current passes through it. The output
energy in the form of heat is forced out of the end of the
hairdryer by the movement of air created by the rotating fan.

This is a very wasteful means of drying hair for once the hot air
leaves the hairdryer only a small amount is used to dry the hair.
The rest escapes into the room, creating an uncomfortable
environment. It would be a more efficient use of energy if more
of the heat from the hairdryer were retained where it is needed,
on the wet hair.

Product evaluation

Product evaluation is an important part of any design-and-
make activity. It is that part of the process that enables you to
reflect on the final outcome. This reflection should be based on
the product specification, for this was the initial requirement
for the design. The product's success or otherwise will now be
judged against the specification.

This focused task is an opportunity for you to practise and develop this skill before starting your major design-and-make project. It is possible to break the product evaluation down into five small sections that should help you through this activity. These are:

1. Select a technology product for evaluation.
2. Measure the performance of the product against specific criteria.
3. Make a critical appraisal of the product.
4. Present your evaluation clearly, logically and concisely.
5. Make realistic proposals for modification.

1 Selecting a technology product for evaluation

Selection: Select a technology product that you use on a regular basis and keep it manageable. Do not try to evaluate the jet engine even though you go on holiday ten times a year. Evaluate something like your watch, an electric kettle or an adjustable reading lamp.

Description: Start by giving a description of the technology product you plan to evaluate and what it does.

Reason for your choice: Say why you have chosen this product to evaluate over all others. It may be because it is used for your hobby, or you have to use it every day in the house.

2 Measuring the performance of the product against specific criteria

'Specific criteria' usually means the specification. You may not have access to the original specification so you will have to try and put yourself in the position of the designer and make a list of what you think the product was designed to do. You will now have to test the product and record your findings. This can be done in the form of a table or short notes.

Case study	Possible specification for an electric kettle

The kettle is shown in Figure 1.8. It is a jug kettle that we mainly use for boiling water to make tea and coffee.

It is my opinion that our electric kettle was designed to do the following:

Figure 1.8 *Electric jug kettle*

Specification

1. Hold 1.7 litres of water.
2. Indicate the level of water in the jug.
3. Be free-standing.
4. Stop when the water is boiled.
5. Be easily filled.
6. Be stable.
7. Pour the water effectively.
8. Be portable.
9. Sell for under £20.00.
10. Safe to use.
11. Boil 1.7 litres of water in under 3 minutes.
12. Be a colour to match the rest of this kitchen equipment range.

3 Make a critical appraisal of the product

One way to do a critical appraisal is to take each of your specification points and comment on how well the product did or did not meet each point.

Example	Electrical jug kettle specification point 6: Be stable

Comment: The kettle has a wide base for stability and four rubber feet to stop it sliding on a wet worktop. The wide base was fine when the kettle was quarter full but when it was filled to the top the centre of gravity was very high. When filled like this it could be toppled over with relative ease. We tend to only fill the kettle half way to avoid this problem.

When the kettle was plugged into the wall the flex became a problem in that it has become an obstacle on the cluttered work surface. Several times there have been near accidents as the kettle was pulled over by the flex getting caught as other equipment was being moved.

5 Modifications

In this section you must suggest and make modifications to the product you are evaluating. These modifications should be based on what you said in section 3. The best way to do this is to make a drawing of the product showing the changes you would make to improve the design. You should annotate your drawing to explain how the changes would make the design or parts of the design better.

Example	Drawing of the modified jug kettle showing some of the changes

- I would make the kettle wider at the base for increased stability.
- I would have an opening lid that opened inside the handle so that my hand was always above and behind the lid. This should help stop the kettle from falling over as you try to pull the lid up.
- I would lower the centre of gravity by making the kettle barrel shaped. This would mean that more water was at the base than at the top.
- I would have the on–off switch close to the top of the handle so that the action is more of a downward push rather than a horizontal push. This would help prevent accidentally pushing the kettle over.
- I would make it from the same materials and change the colour to match the range.

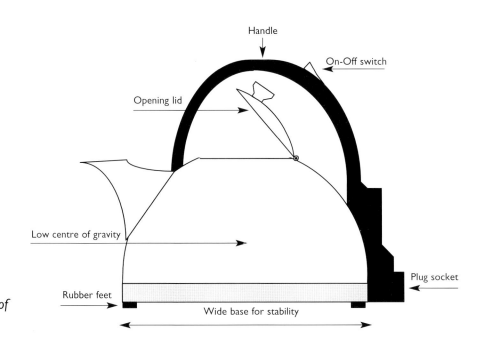

Figure 1.9 *Drawing of the modified kettle*

CHAPTER TWO

Focused Tasks Associated with Communicating

There are three main areas associated with communicating that the following focused tasks are designed to help you with. These are:

1. Computer generated drawing
2. Presentation drawing
3. Dimensioned working drawing (third angle orthographic projection).

CAD (Computer Aided Design)

Computer generated drawings are very useful when you are designing. Possibly the main advantage they have is that they allow you to save a design idea you have drawn and either use it again later or make slight modifications to show the design as it develops. You can also make a library of your drawings or parts of drawings to be used at any time in the future.

CAD is a very wide topic and there are numerous software packages you can buy. All these packages have their own purpose and style that makes them different. You can buy CAD packages for designing electronic circuits, others will draw printed circuit boards, while others are based on a series of pre-drawn clipart shapes that you can bring into a drawing and simply join together to form your drawing.

The purpose of this focused task is to help you draw your own designs from first principles. The software package used throughout this chapter will be **Micrografx Windows Draw 3**. This is an inexpensive and easy to use package found in many schools. However, there are many other similar packages such as Corel Draw or AppleWorks 5 that you can use.

There are a number of skills and techniques associated with CAD. You should be able to:

1. Generate a drawing or part of a drawing from first principles
2. Convey the intended information accurately
3. Employ techniques that are appropriate to the target audience and to the nature of the product
4. Accurately use the graphic tools that are contained in your software package

5. Incorporate elements from a software library in a suitably challenging context.

There are a number of elements you can include in your drawing to demonstrate the above skills and your drawing should include one or more of these. The elements are:

- PCB layout
- circuit diagrams
- working drawings
- packaging graphics associated with a technological product
- charts and graphs.

Figure 2.1 *Ericsson Mobile Phone*

The technological product chosen for this exercise is a mobile phone and its promotional packaging. But it doesn't have to be a phone: it could just as easily be a technology product you made in the past, along with suitable packaging.

Getting started

To do this task you will need either a mobile phone or a picture of one that you can use as resource material for your drawing. The example used here is the Ericsson GA628 mobile phone.

This exercise will show you how to:

- draw and arrange shapes
- create a library of shapes to use in your drawing
- draw types of lines
- add colour to your drawing
- add shading
- group components
- draw a surface development
- add text and convert text to graphics.

Getting to know Micrografx Windows Draw 3

In Micrografx you can draw different types of lines and shapes by selecting them from the top menu bar. You can draw free-hand lines, arcs, pie/pie wedges, polylines, curves, circles, rounded rectangles, rectangles/squares and straight lines. To draw any of these lines click on the draw button (pencil) in the left-hand menu. The top menu will now change to show all the line tools. Figure 2.2 shows you where to find these.

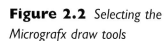

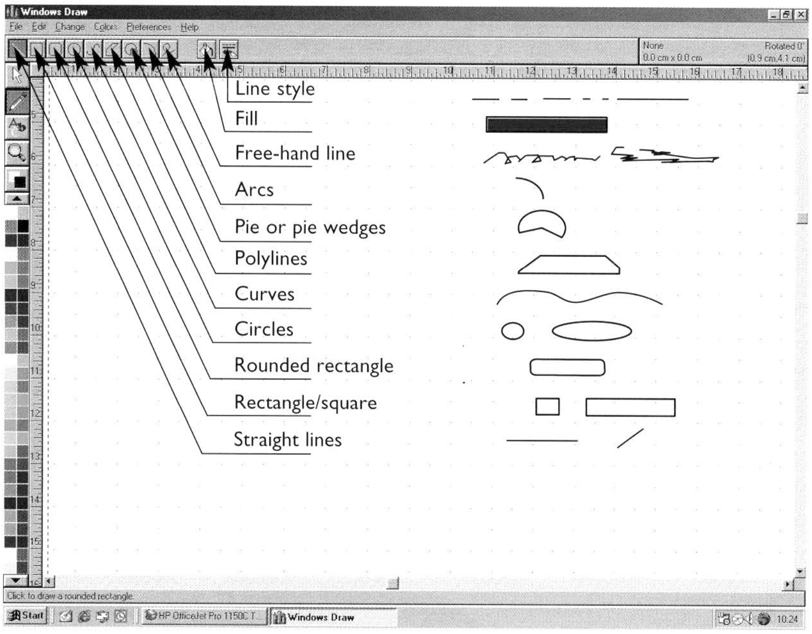

Figure 2.2 *Selecting the Micrografx draw tools*

Figure 2.3 shows where to find the text and other menus on the vertical menu bar.

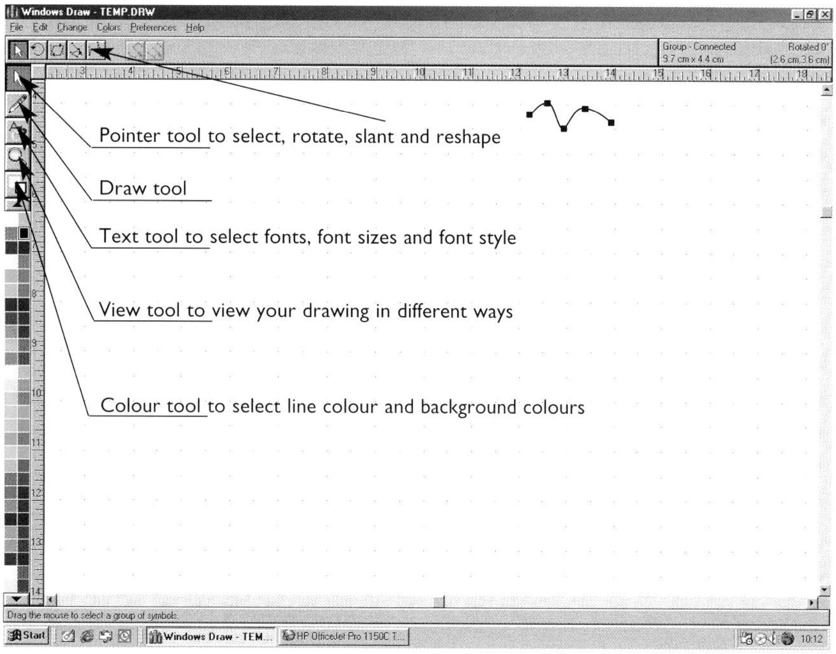

Figure 2.3 *Micrografx vertical menu bar*

The **reshape tool** is useful if the shape you have drawn is not quite correct. To use this tool, click on the drawing you wish to edit. Click on the fourth button along on the pointer menu. This will bring up a series of editing handles. You can pick up one of the editing handles (small black square boxes) at a time and move it around. As you do this you will notice the shape changing.

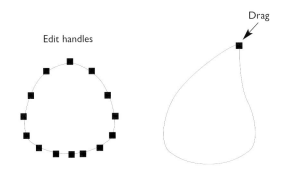

Figure 2.4 *Micrografx pointer tool*

Selecting the phone profile

There are a few basic front profiles that mobile phone makers seem to use. Three of these are shown in Figure 2.5.

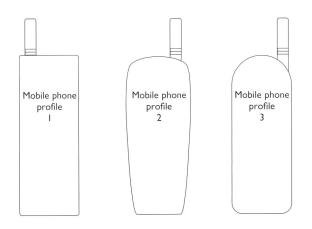

Figure 2.5 *Mobile phone profiles*

Drawing the profiles using Micrografx

When drawing an object that is the same shape on both sides of the centre line (symmetrical), it is good practice to draw one half and then copy and paste it on the other side. This way you are sure that both halves will be the same. Figure 2.6 shows how each profile was drawn.

All three mobile phone profiles were drawn inside a rectangular box. A line was drawn down the middle so that lines and shapes could be positioned on either side of it. This line was removed at the end. The same aerial was used for each profile. The aerial and the cross bands were drawn using the same rounded rectangle tool.

Profile 1

This is the simplest shape and was drawn using the rounded rectangle tool from the top menu bar.

Profile 2

This was the most difficult to draw. One side was drawn using the arc and curve tools. This was then copied, pasted and flipped horizontally to form the other side. The lines were then captured and connected.

Profile 3

One half was drawn using the arc and straight-line tools. This was then copied, pasted and flipped horizontally to form the other side. The lines were then captured and connected.

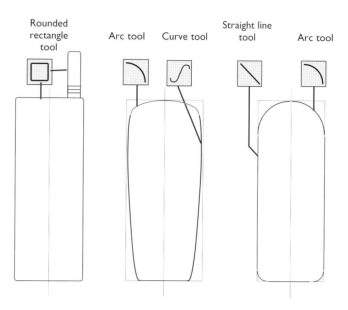

Figure 2.6 *Using the draw tool to draw a profile*

Figure 2.7 *Shading the profile*

Drawing the Ericsson GA628 Mobile Phone

The Ericsson GA628 uses profile 1 shown in Figure 2.5. The drawing of this phone is set out showing the different stages.

Stage 1 Drawing the profile

Draw the profile and connect all lines, if necessary. This should be selected and coloured black (Figure 2.7). If you wish, you can select the gradient from the fill menu and shade the phone black to grey by clicking on the colour palette down the left-hand side.

Stage 2 Drawing the sound recess

Working from the top of the drawing down, draw the sound recess as follows.

Use the arc tool to draw two arcs (Figure 2.8). Copy and paste these before flipping over and joining them to the first two. Next capture all four and go to the drop down menu. Change and select, arrange – connect to join the four arcs. The drawing can now be filled. Finally draw three ovals and drop these on to form the sound holes.

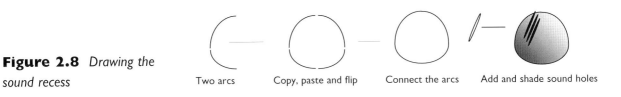

Figure 2.8 *Drawing the sound recess*

Two arcs Copy, paste and flip Connect the arcs Add and shade sound holes

Stage 3 Drawing the display

Draw a rectangle and use the fill/gradient tool to shade it grey-white. Draw the background outline using a polyline and two arcs. Connect these together before filling black. Select the display rectangle and drag it over the background.

Figure 2.9 *Drawing the display*

Filled rectangle Two arcs and polyline Connect and fill Pick and place

Stage 4 Adding the sound recess and display

It is advisable to group your drawing of the sound recess before picking and placing it close to the top of the phone profile.

Do the same with the display drawing before picking and placing it on the profile. Make sure it is centred on the centre line.

Draw a small oval and fill it green. This will be the charging light. Place it on the profile before sending it to the back (Figure 2.10).

Stage 5 Drawing the buttons

The yes/no buttons are the same shape as the sound recess so copy this and reduce it in size to act as a button. The number buttons are all one unfilled oval outside and one solid oval inside. You will need 15, so simply draw one and copy it 15 times for all the numbers and functions.

Charging light

Figure 2.10 *Placing the drawing on the profile*

Figure 2.11 *Drawing the buttons*

Stage 6 Adding text to the buttons

Select the text menu from the left-hand menu bar. Next select a font. Micrografx always defaults to *Swiss* but this is not a true font so you will have to select one from the drop down menu.

Figure 2.12 *Button panel*

Final drawing of Ericsson GA628 mobile phone

Place the number on your button and change the colour to white before grouping.

Draw a rectangular button panel and locate the buttons on it. Group the finished button panel before picking and placing on the phone profile.

Stage 7 Adding text to the drawing

To add the white texts simply select text from the menu and type the name. Now select white from the colour palette and click on it. The text will change to that colour. Pick and place this on your phone profile. Your drawing should now look like the diagram below.

Mobile phone packaging

To complete the CAD focused task on the Ericsson mobile phone you need to design a sales package. The package can take many forms, such as:

- a folded cardboard box with the phone inside
- a clear plastic blister pack through which you can see the phone
- a coloured polyethylene bag.

You only have to look at how similar products are packaged to find inspiration for this part of the task.

The example shown in Figure 2.13 is the surface development of a packaging in which the Ericsson mobile phone could be sold. The box has the appropriate advertising and product information on the outer surfaces. The good thing about this part of the task is that you can use all or part of your CAD drawing as a series of library components that can be pasted onto the packaging.

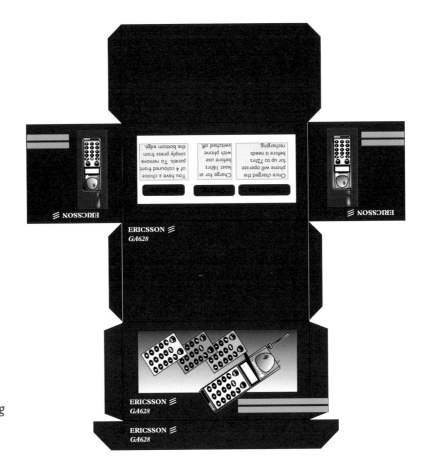

Figure 2.13 *Packaging for the Ericsson GA628 mobile phone*

Presentation Drawing

Sketching and drawing are central to designing. They are the means by which you explain and record your thinking as you struggle to find a solution to your problem. A presentation drawing is the final stage of this process. It is a quality drawing that allows you to show what your final idea will look like.

This focused task is an opportunity for you to practise and develop this skill should you wish to do so. It is possible to break the focused task down into five sections that should help guide you through the activity. These are:

1. Select a technological product and produce a pictorial drawing. The drawing can be in either 2D or 3D.
2. Employ techniques which are appropriate to your selected product.
3. On the drawing, demonstrate rendering skills using appropriate media (e.g. line, pattern, texture, tone and colour in coloured pencils or watercolour or markers, or on a computer).
4. Demonstrate a good understanding of scale and proportion in your drawing.
5. Use annotation where appropriate on the drawing.

When practising a presentation drawing, select a product which reflects the type of product you are likely to be drawing in your major project. Remember you are developing a skill you will need for this, so select a product of similar complexity. Don't attempt to draw a Formula 1 racing car when all you are likely to design is a security system, an aid for the disabled or a lifting mechanism.

Two-dimensional (2D) drawing

By drawing one or more flat two-dimensional (2D) views of a technological product and using coloured pencils, pastel chalks, dry markers or a mixture of all three, it is possible to shade and texture your drawing to make it appear three-dimensional (3D).

When attempting pictorial drawing for the first time it is a good idea to start with one or two 2D views of the product as shown in Figure 2.14. These can then be rendered to give the drawing the desired impact. By doing this you will become more familiar with the product. This knowledge can then be used to generate a 3D drawing of the product if you so desire.

| **Case study** | **2D presentation drawing of a moisture probe** |

A pencil drawing was made of the electronic moisture probe before using coloured pencils to add shade and texture to enhance the drawing. The next stage was to attempt the drawing in 3D.

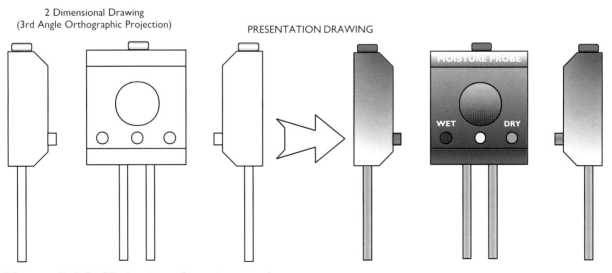

Figure 2.14 *2D drawings of a moisture probe*

Drawing the moisture probe in 3D

The technique used in Figure 2.15 was isometric projection. In this method, the sloping lines are drawn at 30 degrees to the horizontal as shown. The isometric circles were drawn using an isometric ellipse drawing template.

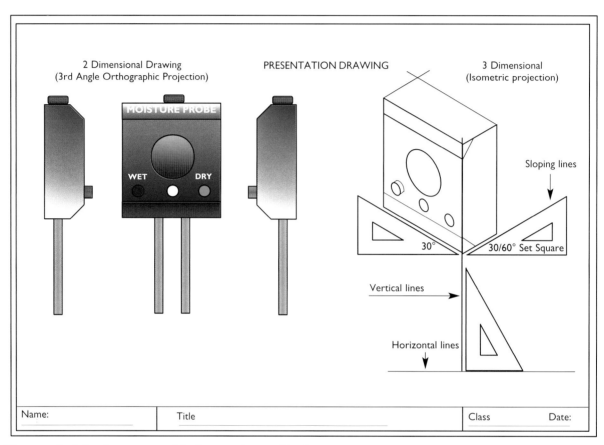

Figure 2.15 *Generating a 3D drawing from a 2D drawing*

Adding colour to the isometric drawing of the moisture probe

By using coloured pencils you can add colour and shading to a 3D view. The technique involves holding the pencil on its side to lay down more colour with a single pass. By making repeated passes over the same area you can add depth to the colour. This will give the effect of shading. A black pencil can be used to form a shadow under the drawing. Finally a white pencil can be used to highlight the edges. The coloured pencils used were Derwent Artists Pencils. These or similar artist's pencils give a good coverage and depth of colour.

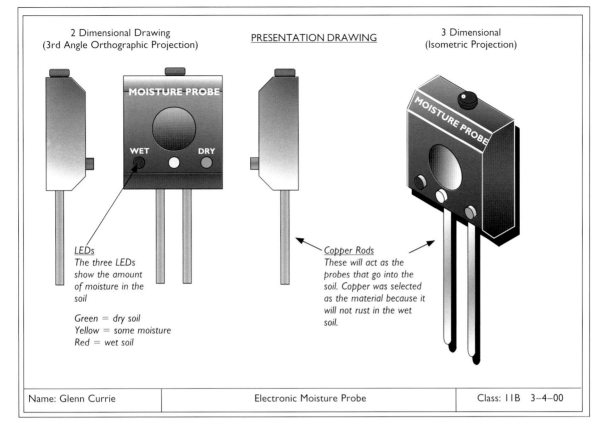

Inside the figure:

2 Dimensional Drawing
(3rd Angle Orthographic Projection)

PRESENTATION DRAWING

3 Dimensional
(Isometric Projection)

MOISTURE PROBE

WET   DRY

MOISTURE PROBE

LEDs
The three LEDs
show the amount
of moisture in the
soil

Green = dry soil
Yellow = some moisture
Red = wet soil

Copper Rods
These will act as the
probes that go into the
soil. Copper was selected
as the material because it
will not rust in the wet
soil.

| Name: Glenn Currie | Electronic Moisture Probe | Class: 11B   3–4–00 |

Figure 2.16 *Final 2D and 3D drawing of the moisture probe*

Adding annotations to your drawings

To annotate a drawing means to add short explanatory notes to it. The purpose of annotation is to provide more information about your design. The presentation drawing in Figure 2.16 has some annotations added to explain the purpose of the LEDs and the material used for the probes.

Dry markers

The dry marker is a fast drying spirit-based marker. While it takes a little bit of getting used to, the final results are more striking than coloured pencils. The two markers that students seem to get the most success with are the Edding 2000/2200 grafix permanent art markers and the Pantone. For everyday school use, the Edding are a good all-round choice. They are fast drying, refillable and give off a low odour.

The technique of using markers

The technique involves using a chisel point marker to lay down a strip of coloured ink, leaving this to dry then laying down another layer on top. The more passes over the same line the deeper the colour will become. This process will add shade and texture to your presentation drawing.

The steps necessary to complete a dry marker rendering of your drawing are:

1. Make a light 2D pencil drawing of the technological product.
2. Make a photocopy. This way you can practise the technique.
3. Select the light colours first. If necessary it is then possible to go over this with a dark colour.
4. Using a chisel point marker lay down the foundation colour. Use a 'T' square and make these lines all run in the same direction. Don't worry about running past the outside edges of the drawing.
5. Decide on which direction the light is falling on your product. By making another pass with the same marker you can start to darken the areas in shadow. The more passes you make the deeper the colour will appear. This is shown in Figure 2.17.
6. Use a white coloured pencil to add highlights. The Berol Karisma white 938 is a good pencil for this job.
7. Use a black pen to outline your drawing.
8. When completely dry, place the drawing on a cutting mat. Using a sharp craft knife and safety rule cut around the outside of the drawing. Finally paste the drawing on to your presentation page. A completed example of a cordless drill is shown in Figure 2.18.

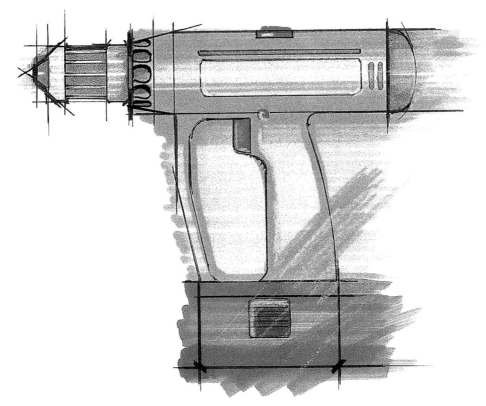

Figure 2.17 *Dry marker drawing of a cordless drill*

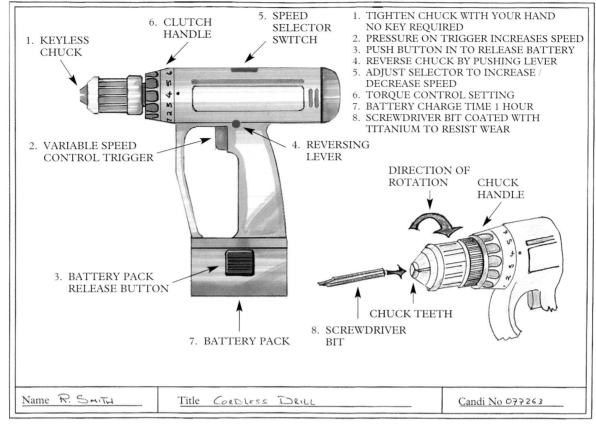

1. KEYLESS CHUCK

6. CLUTCH HANDLE

5. SPEED SELECTOR SWITCH

1. TIGHTEN CHUCK WITH YOUR HAND NO KEY REQUIRED
2. PRESSURE ON TRIGGER INCREASES SPEED
3. PUSH BUTTON IN TO RELEASE BATTERY
4. REVERSE CHUCK BY PUSHING LEVER
5. ADJUST SELECTOR TO INCREASE / DECREASE SPEED
6. TORQUE CONTROL SETTING
7. BATTERY CHARGE TIME 1 HOUR
8. SCREWDRIVER BIT COATED WITH TITANIUM TO RESIST WEAR

2. VARIABLE SPEED CONTROL TRIGGER

4. REVERSING LEVER

DIRECTION OF ROTATION

CHUCK HANDLE

3. BATTERY PACK RELEASE BUTTON

CHUCK TEETH

7. BATTERY PACK

8. SCREWDRIVER BIT

Name R. Smith   Title Cordless Drill   Candi No 077263

Figure 2.18 *Dry marker rendering of a cordless drill*

Figure 2.18 shows the final presentation drawing for the cordless drill. Additional information has been added in the form of annotation and a 3D drawing of the chuck.

Examples

Some examples of presentation drawings are shown in Figures 2.19 and 2.20.

The circular saw shown in Figure 2.19 was rendered in a mix of dry markers and coloured pencils. The drawing and the typed annotations were cut and pasted on to a drawing page before being colour photocopied to give the final overall presentation.

Figure 2.20 shows a student's 3D presentation drawing of a mains powered jigsaw. The jigsaw was rendered using coloured pencil. The use of background shading makes the drawing more striking, enabling it to stand out on the page.

The use of enlargements to show the method of holding the blade added to the overall presentation.

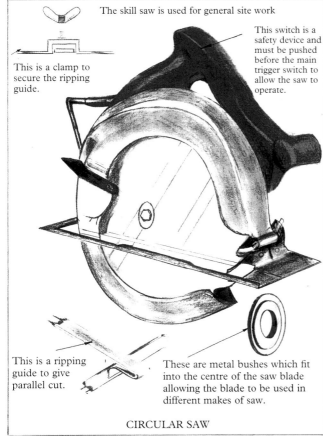

The skill saw is used for general site work

This switch is a safety device and must be pushed before the main trigger switch to allow the saw to operate.

This is a clamp to secure the ripping guide.

This is a ripping guide to give parallel cut.

These are metal bushes which fit into the centre of the saw blade allowing the blade to be used in different makes of saw.

CIRCULAR SAW

Figure 2.19 *Presentation drawing of a circular saw*

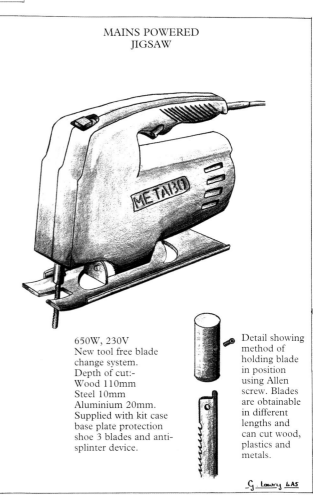

MAINS POWERED
JIGSAW

METABO

650W, 230V
New tool free blade change system.
Depth of cut:-
Wood 110mm
Steel 10mm
Aluminium 20mm.
Supplied with kit case base plate protection shoe 3 blades and anti-splinter device.

Detail showing method of holding blade in position using Allen screw. Blades are obtainable in different lengths and can cut wood, plastics and metals.

G Lowry LAS

Figure 2.20 *Presentation drawing of a jigsaw*

Dimensioned Working Drawing

A dimensioned working drawing is an important part of any design. It enables you to add precise dimensions to the product you have just designed. This should speed up the manufacturing process as well as ensuring all the different parts fit at the assembly stage.

Every part of a working drawing must conform to a common standard called the **ISO standard**. This will ensure that anyone looking at your drawing will know precisely what it shows. The type of drawing you will be doing in this focused task is called **orthographic projection**.

This focused task is an opportunity for you to practise and develop these skills before starting your major design-and-make project activity.

Orthographic projection

Orthographic projection is a standard method of drawing where you draw a number of flat views of your project looking from the front, top and side. The drawing is normally drawn to scale. The number of views and the order in which you show them is also important. For example, Figure 2.21(a) shows the top view of a wood joint. The top view alone has insufficient information for anyone to know precisely which joint it is. If on the other hand you add a second view looking in from the front, as shown in Figure 2.21(b), the joint starts to become clear.

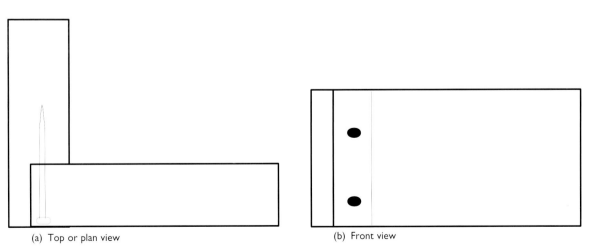

(a) Top or plan view

(b) Front view

Figure 2.21 *Wood joint*

Adding dimensions

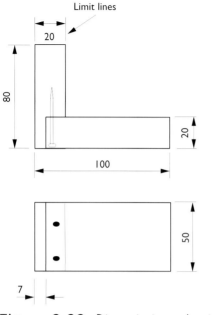

Limit lines

20

80

20

100

50

7

Figure 2.22 *Dimensioning a drawing*

The wood joint shown in Figure 2.21 may be recognisable as a joint called an end lap but you would still be unable to make it from just these drawings. You would need to know the dimensions of each piece. Figure 2.22 shows the same wood joint with dimensions added. It would now be possible to mark out and make the joint.

Dimensions should conform to the following:

- Dimension lines should be drawn slightly lighter in weight than the drawing.
- Dimensions should be above or at right angles to the lines but not resting on it.
- Dimension limit lines must indicate the full length of the dimension line and extend out from but not touch the drawing.
- Arrowheads must be closed. They must also touch the dimension limit lines.

Third-angle orthographic projection

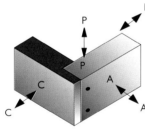

Figure 2.23 *Pictorial view*

Third-angle orthographic projection has to a large extent replaced first-angle throughout Europe. Therefore presentation drawings should now conform to this standard.

If you consider the pictorial drawing of a joint shown in Figure 2.23 you will notice four of the faces have the letters A, B, C and P on them. This drawing will be used to explain third-angle projection.

Third-angle orthographic projection has the side view appearing next to the front view on the drawing.

You should start by looking at the joint from the front, view A, and take this as your first view. This is called the **front elevation**.

Now go above the joint and look down on the top, P. What you see is called the **plan** and this view must be drawn above the front elevation.

If you then look at the right-hand side, B, what you see must be drawn beside the front elevation, on the right. This is called the **side elevation**. The left-hand side C would then be drawn to the left as shown. When drawing in third-angle projection it is common practice to draw both end views.

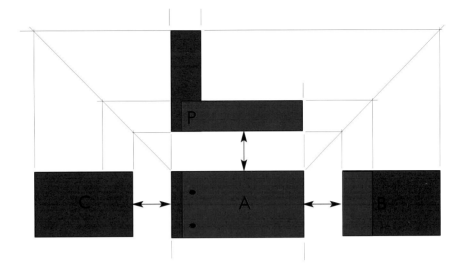

Figure 2.24 *Third-angle orthographic projection*

The correct way to present a third-angle orthographic drawing is to draw the views using a 2H pencil or pen and ink. You must not use colour or shading on your drawing.

Drawing lines: These are the lines used for the actual drawing. They must be drawn heavier than dimension lines.

Projection and construction lines: These are light lines used during the construction of the drawing. They should be removed from the final drawing.

Hidden detail lines: These are light dotted lines that show parts of the object that are hidden behind others.

Third-angle symbol: This is shown at the top of Figure 2.25.

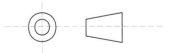

Symbol for 3rd Angle

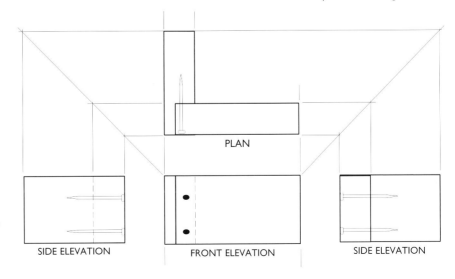

PLAN

Figure 2.25 *Third-angle orthographic drawing of an end lap joint*

SIDE ELEVATION   FRONT ELEVATION   SIDE ELEVATION

A third-angle orthographic projection working drawing

If you have selected a working drawing as your focused task you can use either conventional pencil and paper or a CAD package to produce your drawing. It is a good idea to draw a technology product that you are familiar with. The example shown in Figure 2.26 was a year 9 mechanisms project.

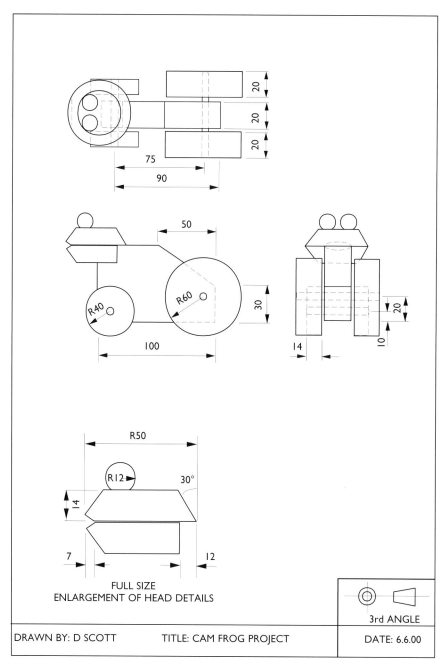

DRAWN BY: D SCOTT   TITLE: CAM FROG PROJECT   DATE: 6.6.00

Figure 2.26 *Working drawing of a cam-operated frog*

CHAPTER THREE   Design projects

As a technology and design student you will be required to design and manufacture a product that involves energy and control. The choice of project will be made by you in consultation with your teacher and should reflect the content of the syllabus.

You have to submit a product you have manufactured, accompanied by its portfolio.

It is this part of your GCSE that will attract the most marks. You can be awarded up to 50% of the total marks for this part of the course so it is well worth your while putting time and effort into it. The common elements in all design projects, regardless of tier, are:

- designing
- communicating
- manufacture
- using energy and control.

Elements of designing

While there is no single design process that will guide you through every design problem to the ultimate solution, there are a number of common elements that appear in most technology and design projects. The order in which you consider and address each of these elements will change from project to project.

What is common to all technology and design projects is the constant going back to earlier elements of your work to monitor and evaluate what you are doing. Some refer to this as the circular nature of design: the constant going round and round until you arrive at the best possible solution.

You can think of the design process as a giant wheel. At its centre is the activity of designing. Around the outer edges are all the activities associated with it. You are constantly going out to these activities in order to undertake specific tasks which you bring back into your central activity of designing. A design wheel is shown in Figure 3.1.

Figure 3.1 *Design elements*

Design portfolio

The portfolio will contain your design work. It should include evidence of your ability to investigate, generate, evaluate, communicate and use energy and control.

The portfolio should contain quality work not quantity. It should be summative in nature. That is, as you think something through you should record your thinking in the form of sketches and notes. You should include important research and investigation material. You should show evidence of constant evaluation and modification to your evolving designs.

Situations

You should consider a small number of situations before selecting one for further research and investigation. Chapter 1 covers the topic of situations and gives examples of a pupil's work. If you are unsure as to what is required in this section it may be worth referring to this chapter.

Design brief

The brief is a short written statement of what you plan to design and make. It should be open-ended. One example of an open-ended design brief for an aid for the disabled is: 'Design and manufacture a device to assist my elderly arthritic grandparents remove a lid from commonly used screw capped jars'.

This describes what you plan to design and make but leaves the design options open to a number of possible solutions.

Research and investigation of the chosen situation

This section of your portfolio is where you show evidence that you have carried out research and investigation into the chosen situation. One way to do this is to take a few photographs that you can refer too. More information on this element of the design process can be found in Chapter 1.

Initial specification

The initial specification is a list of short statements listing what the client or end user wants your final product to do or have. The initial specification is important; it will be central to all your early thinking. It is also one of the means by which your final project will be judged. At this stage of design it is not possible to be precise about what you want from the product; this will come later when you have arrived at a possible solution. Only then can you put precise boundaries on the performance you expect from your final product in the form of a final specification.

In industry the initial specification usually comes from the client and may be a few lines to one page long. The final specification comes from the manufacturing team after some research and development and will be drawn up in consultation with the client and end user. Final industrial specifications could be up to fifty pages long and cover every component and all the materials used in the product.

Example

This was an initial specification from a student who was asked to design and manufacture a device to assist her elderly arthritic grandparents remove a lid from commonly used screw capped jars.

The product should:

1. remove a lid from a range of jars
2. be used by both grandparents
3. cost no more than £15.00
4. be freestanding on the kitchen worktop
5. be a device that is able help the grandparents overcome their disability
6. be easily cleaned in case of spillage
7. hold one jar at a time.

Research and investigation of the initial specification

This section of your portfolio should be based on the initial specification. It will provide you with the opportunity to find out more details about the problem. This should help you at the next stage of the process, producing possible solutions in the form of concept sketches.

If you consider the initial specification for the example given above, then your task would be to research and investigate each of these points to find out as much information as possible before starting on your concept sketches.

For example: 'Point 1. Remove a lid from a range of jars'.

You should find out the sizes of the lids in the range. So before you could start sketching solutions you would need to measure the size of the lids and jars that are commonly used.

Concept sketches

These are at the very core of designing. They should show what you are thinking as you struggle for the best solution. They should be quick freehand sketches that occasionally have colour added to highlight a good idea or part of an idea.

Ideas for concept sketches

If you are having difficulty finding different ideas for your concept sketches you could apply the technique of using different technologies to find different solutions. For instance, in the following example, if the student working on the problem of an aid for her arthritic grandparents to assist them with the opening of jars had considered a pneumatic, electronic or even a microprocessor solution, then there may have been a possible alternative solution in one or more of these systems. If you consider the pneumatic solution you may think this is impractical, but it is not as impractical as it may at first seem for it is possible to buy a quiet pneumatic compressor smaller than a bag of sugar. This could then be incorporated into the final design.

Example

Figure 3.2 shows a page of concept sketches from a student's portfolio on an aid for her arthritic grandparents. The sketches are freehand and spontaneous and are a summary of the student's thinking.

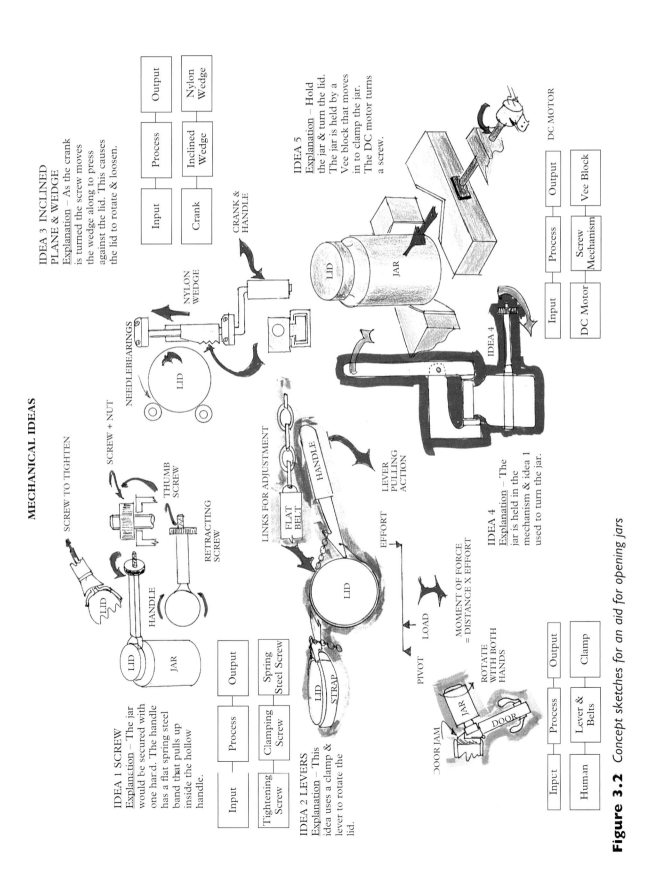

Figure 3.2 *Concept sketches for an aid for opening jars*

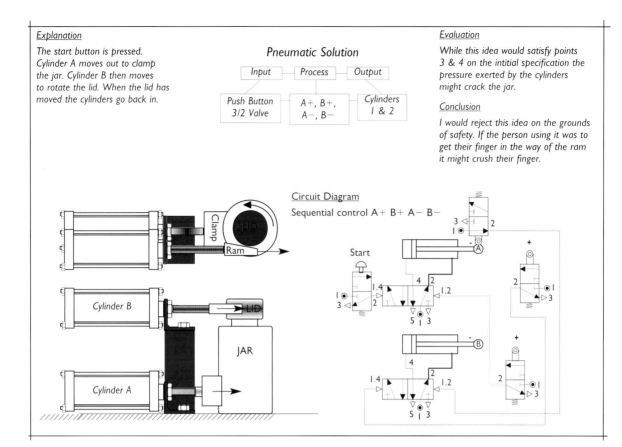

Explanation

The start button is pressed. Cylinder A moves out to clamp the jar. Cylinder B then moves to rotate the lid. When the lid has moved the cylinders go back in.

Pneumatic Solution

Input — Process — Output

Push Button 3/2 Valve | A+, B+, A−, B− | Cylinders 1 & 2

Evaluation

While this idea would satisfy points 3 & 4 on the intitial specification the pressure exerted by the cylinders might crack the jar.

Conclusion

I would reject this idea on the grounds of safety. If the person using it was to get their finger in the way of the ram it might crush their finger.

Circuit Diagram
Sequential control A+ B+ A− B−

Figure 3.3 *Concept drawing using CAD of a pneumatic device to open jars*

Using CAD to generate concept drawings

If you feel that your sketching skills are not up to standard and you have spent time developing good CAD skills, it is possible to use these skills to generate concept drawings. Figure 3.3 shows how CAD could be used to generate concept drawings for a pneumatic solution to the design problem 'aid for the disabled'.

Selecting your best idea from your concept sketches

From your range of concept sketches/drawings you will have to select one idea for further development. As well as selecting your best or most suitable idea you will have to justify your selection. This is important, as this selection will become the basis for the development of the chosen idea later in your portfolio.

Detailed specification

Following the selection of your chosen idea you should be in position to say what precisely you want this idea to do or have. This final list is set out as a detailed specification. Many of the original points set out in your initial specification may or may not be in your detailed specification.

The detailed specification is important. It is this that you will use to evaluate your product after it is manufactured and tested. The detailed specification should include such things as the:

- performance of the product
- ergonomics
- final product cost
- materials the product should be made from
- finish
- servicing
- dimensions
- parameters for the system you plan to use, e.g. electronic timer to come on once every ten minutes or a gearbox with a speed of 25 revs/min.

Development of the chosen idea

You should now be in a position to develop your chosen idea through to a final project.

The development is likely to include a section on each of the following:

- development of the system
- development of the product housing or unit
- a presentation drawing
- a working drawing or sketch
- a cutting list/bill of materials
- a plan for manufacture.

Development of the system

You will have to incorporate energy and control into your product. If your chosen idea incorporates electronics it is good practice to develop this first before you start to design the casing. In this way you will be sure that the circuit will fit inside your design. If you are using mechanisms in your final design the mechanism itself may well be the final system and product. But in either case it is a good practice to start with a simple system and keep developing it until you have your final system.

Development of a system to control a rotating CD storage unit

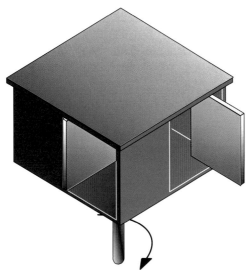

Figure 3.4 *Rotating CD storage unit*

The project shown in Figure 3.4 is a rotating CD storage unit that a student designed for GCSE Technology and Design. The unit had to hold 40 CDs. As some of these would be behind others, the unit had to rotate through 90° at a time. The final system was in two parts:

1. electronic system to turn on a DC motor for a set time
2. mechanical system to turn the unit at the correct speed.

Figure 3.5 shows the development of the system.

1 Electronics

The electronic system started out as a simple circuit incorporating a motor, battery and push-to-make switch, and concluded with a RS flip-flop with output to a relay.

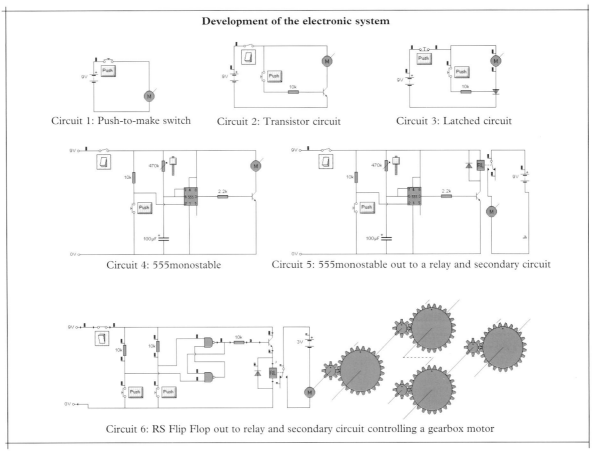

Figure 3.5 *Developing the system*

2 Mechanisms

A relay was used to turn the final drive system, which incorporated a gearbox motor, pulleys and belt. This system was developed around a simple gearbox motor unit which had a series of plastic gears that could be assembled to give different gear ratios.

The student was given the speed of the motor in revs/min and a number of different gear wheels. From this, the student was able to calculate a suitable output speed for the final drive shaft of 22 revs/min. This was finally reduced by a ratio of 4:1 by using a belt and pulley system. The final output speed of the rotating storage unit was approximately 6 revs/min.

Some of the students development work for the gearbox is shown in Figure 3.6.

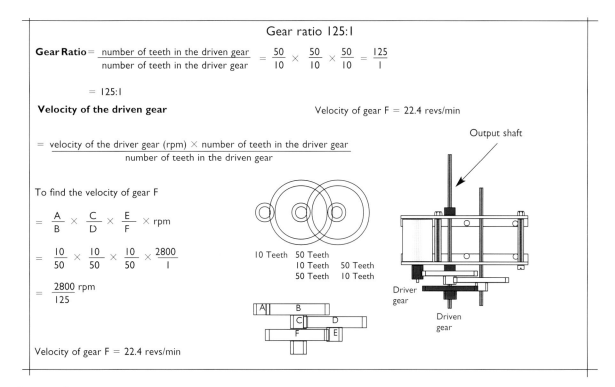

Figure 3.6 *Developing the mechanical system*

Development of the product housing for your system

Having developed a system such as electronics or the Peripheral Interface Controller (PIC) you will need to incorporate this into your product. Keep this in mind as your design develops.

You should now use a range of concept sketches to explore different product casing designs.

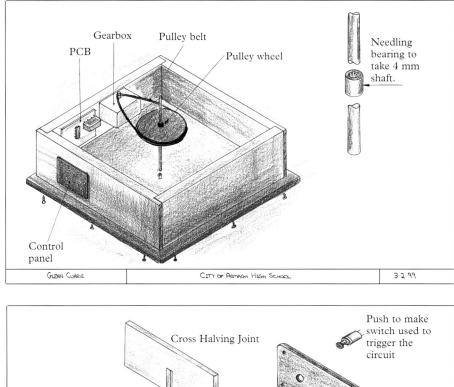

Needling
bearing to
take 4 mm
shaft.

Pulley belt

Gearbox

PCB

Pulley wheel

Control
panel

GLENN CURRIE   CITY OF ARMAGH HIGH SCHOOL   3·2·99

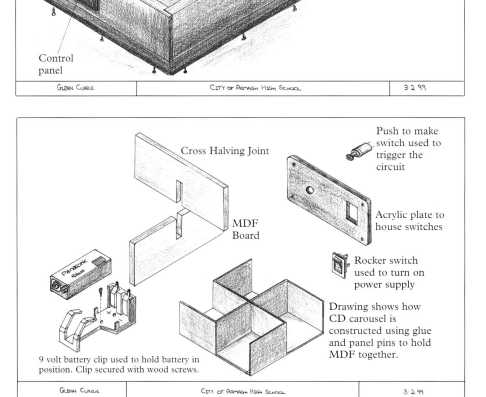

Cross Halving Joint

MDF
Board

Push to make
switch used to
trigger the
circuit

Acrylic plate to
house switches

Rocker switch
used to turn on
power supply

Drawing shows how
CD carousel is
constructed using glue
and panel pins to hold
MDF together.

9 volt battery clip used to hold battery in
position. Clip secured with wood screws.

GLENN CURRIE   CITY OF ARMAGH HIGH SCHOOL   3·2·99

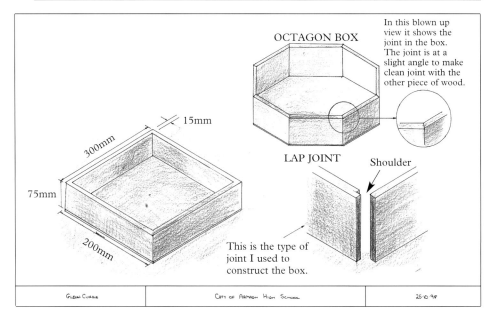

OCTAGON BOX

In this blown up
view it shows the
joint in the box.
The joint is at a
slight angle to make
clean joint with the
other piece of wood.

15mm

300mm

75mm

200mm

LAP JOINT   Shoulder

This is the type of
joint I used to
construct the box.

GLENN CURRIE   CITY OF ARMAGH HIGH SCHOOL   25·10·98

Figure 3.7 *Developing the chosen idea*

It is at this stage that sketches will include such information as:

- construction details
- dimensions
- servicing details
- type finish
- choice of materials.

As this work progresses, and if it is appropriate, you should evaluate your work against your final specification to ensure a best fit at all times.

Example

Figure 3.7 shows extracts from a student's portfolio showing some development work for the rotating CD storage unit.

Manufacture

Working drawing

The working drawing should contain enough information to enable you or others to manufacture your design. The drawing can be either a dimensioned sketch or an orthographic drawing.

If you choose to do your working drawing in orthographic projection then this should be in third-angle projection. Third-angle orthographic projection is explained in detail in Chapter 2. It may be worth reading this section before attempting this part of your portfolio.

Example

Figure 3.8 shows an extract from a student's portfolio. It shows the working drawing in third-angle for his rotating CD storage unit.

Material cutting list

This is a list of all the materials you will need to manufacture your product. You should set out your cutting list in a precise way so that others will understand it. The correct way to do this is shown in Table 3.1. This is a cutting list for the rotating CD storage unit.

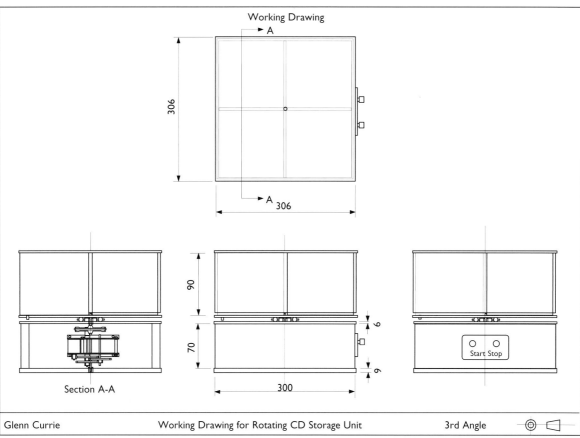

Working Drawing

Section A-A

Glenn Currie · Working Drawing for Rotating CD Storage Unit · 3rd Angle

Figure 3.8 *Working drawing for the rotating CD storage unit*

Table 3.1 *Materials cutting list for the rotating CD storage unit*

Part	Number	Length	Width	Thickness	Material
Base Unit					
L.Side	2	300	70	20	Pine
R.Side	2	288	70	20	Pine
Motor Plate	1	260	70	14	Pine
Base	1	306	306	9	MDF
Top	1	306	306	5	Acrylic
Storage Unit					
Sides	4	153	90	6	MDF
Top	1	306	306	6	MDF
Bottom	1	306	306	6	MDF
Middle	2	288	90	6	MDF

Manufacturing plan

This is a plan showing the sequence in which you plan to manufacture your project.

Most students set this out as a list that is written in the sequence in which you will manufacture it. It is also possible to set out a manufacturing plan as a flowchart. An example of part of a flowchart for the rotating CD storage unit is shown in Figure 3.9.

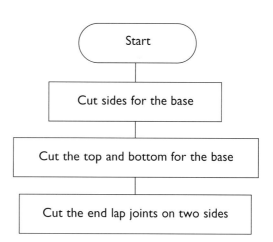

Figure 3.9

Manufacturing plan

Evaluation of the product

Evaluation of the product will be an ongoing process throughout the design and manufacture, and comments should be made as this work progresses. You will also need to evaluate the final outcome after you have made and tested it. This entails returning to your detailed specification and design brief and commenting on how well you feel your final product satisfies these.

You should start your evaluation by testing your product against as many points in the detailed specification as you can. You can do this in written form or in table form where you set down the points in one column and your findings in another. Try to be critical in your remarks on how well your product satisfied each point. Product evaluation is explained in detail in Chapter 1. You may wish to refer to this before starting on this section. Extracts from a student's product evaluation for a CD rotating storage unit are shown below.

Specification point 1: The unit must turn through 90 degrees and stop

Test results: At first it worked fine but after a few weeks, as the battery ran down, it would stop before the 90 degrees.

Critical appraisal: This became a constant source of annoyance, as I could not always see the titles on the CD. The problem was solved when I fitted a jack plus socket and connected in an old unused power supply.

Specification point 2: The unit should move slowly and quietly

Test results: The unit was geared down to a 625:1 ratio, which enables it to turn slowly, but the gearbox was found to be very noisy.

Critical appraisal: The speed of rotation was fine but the noise was a constant source of annoyance. I was never really able to solve this problem although when I oiled the gears it improved. If I were to make the unit again I would use a better quality gearbox, which tend to run more quietly.

Specification point 3: Battery operated circuit

Test results: A 9 volt PP3 battery powered the circuit for the project. While the circuit worked well for a time using the PP3 battery, this needs to be charged every few weeks to ensure the smooth working of the project.

Critical appraisal: A problem I can see with this is the expense of buying batteries and the trouble I will have when I go to change the battery. The problem was solved when I fitted the jack plug and used a 9 volt external power supply. The battery was left connected to the project as a back-up power source.

Modifications to the product

Every product, no matter how well it is made, can be improved upon. In this section of your portfolio you have the opportunity to say what you would change to improve your design. Where appropriate you should include sketches of any modification you would make.

An example of part of a product modification for the rotating CD storage unit is shown in Figure 3.10.

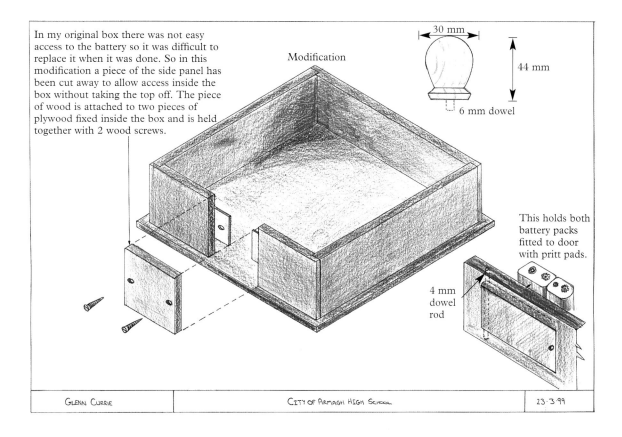

In my original box there was not easy access to the battery so it was difficult to replace it when it was done. So in this modification a piece of the side panel has been cut away to allow access inside the box without taking the top off. The piece of wood is attached to two pieces of plywood fixed inside the box and is held together with 2 wood screws.

Modification

30 mm

44 mm

6 mm dowel

This holds both battery packs fitted to door with pritt pads.

4 mm dowel rod

GLENN CURRIE   CITY OF ARMAGH HIGH SCHOOL   23·3·99

Figure 3.10

Modifications to the final product, the addition of a battery box

CHAPTER FOUR **Materials**

Timber

For thousands of years, trees have been used to make wooden products and this is still true today. Timber has become one of our managed natural resources and is used all around the home. In technology it is used to make such things as mechanical toys, housings for electronic circuits and in mould making for vacuum forming plastics.

Deciduous trees include hardwoods such as beech and mahogany. You can recognise deciduous trees in summer as they nearly all have broad leaves. During the winter these leaves fall off.

Conifers include softwoods such as pine and cedar. You can recognise softwood trees as they have needles instead of broad leaves. Most softwood trees are evergreens which means they keep their needles all the year round.

Figure 4.1 *Hardwood tree*

Figure 4.2 *Softwood tree*

From trees to planks
Felling

Trees are growing, living structures. They take in water and nutrients from the soil and transport it to the leaves. In the leaves, energy from sunlight converts water and carbon dioxide from the air into plant food. As this process happens during the summer months, trees are usually cut down in the non-growing season.

The tree is felled and the trunk cut into logs 4–6 m long. The logs are then transported to the sawmill where the bark is removed and they are cut into planks.

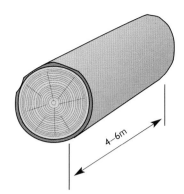

Figure 4.3 *Logs 4–6 m long*

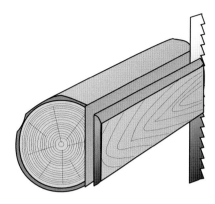

Figure 4.4 *Logs are cut into planks*

Seasoning

The planks are left to dry before they are finally sawn into planks for sale to the public. The drying process is called seasoning and can take between 6 months and 2 years if the timber is left outside. The process can be speeded-up if the wet planks are placed in a hot building called a kiln. Kiln drying takes 1–3 weeks.

Conversion

Conversion is the term given to sawing logs into planks. There are two main methods of doing this:

1. plain sawing
2. quarter sawing.

Plain sawing is quick and cheap to do but some planks will warp more than others. Figure 4.5 shows two planks; the centre one is the most desirable, as it tends to warp very little, while the lower plank will warp a lot. Wet planks have a tendency to bend away from the heart as they dry out.

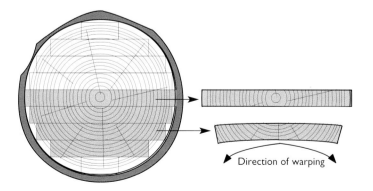

Figure 4.5 *Plain sawn log*

Quarter sawing is slow and expensive to do and is usually only used for expensive hardwoods such as mahogany. Planks cut in this way tend to warp less than plain sawn ones because the growth rings are across the plank as show in Figure 4.6.

47

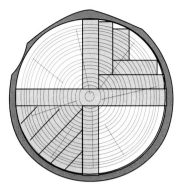

Figure 4.6 *Two methods of quarter sawing*

Quarter sawing refers to either of the two methods shown in Figure 4.6. The lower, radial, method is the most expensive and tends to be reserved for special hardwoods such as oak.

Common sizes of planks

Planks can be purchased in common sizes. This means that when you a buy a plank today, next week, next month or next year it will always have the same dimensions. Planks are sold as either rough or finished (planed) planks. Some of the common finished sizes are shown in Table 4.1.

Table 4.1 *Common sizes of planks*

Width (mm)	Finished thickness in millimetres				
	12	16	19	32	44
19	x	x	x		
32	x	x	x	x	
44	x	x	x	x	x
69	x	x	x	x	x
94	x	x	x	x	x
119		x	x	x	x
144			x	x	x
169			x	x	x
194			x	x	x
219			x	x	x

Grain

Grain is the term given to the pattern of the wood. These patterns are made by the growth rings of the tree. Figure 4.7 shows the end grain, surface grain and side grain on a piece of wood.

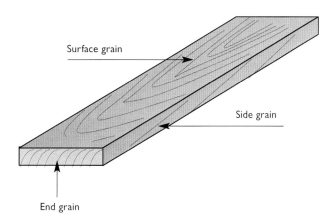

Figure 4.7 *Grain lines*

Surface grain

Side grain

End grain

Properties of wood

The structure of a tree as it grows allows nutrients to travel up and down the trunk to keep it alive. This structure is a series of short bonded tubes called cells. If you looked at them under a microscope they would look like small drinking straws. It is this tubular structure that gives timber its strength.

The tubes or cells are larger towards the outside edges of the trunk, so during seasoning they shrink more than the cells in the middle. This is why timber tends to warp.

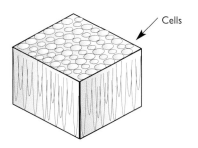

Cells

Figure 4.8 *Structure of wood*

Mechanical properties of timber

Because timber has cells arranged in bundles, it may help you to think of a plank as a bundle of straws, and imagine how it will react to different forces.

Tension along the grain
Timber will be strong in tension along its length, that is, it can resist large pulling forces (Figure 4.9).

Compression down the grain
While timber is good at resisting compression forces applied to each end it is not as good in compression as it is in tension. A piece of timber could be up to 50% weaker in compression than in tension.

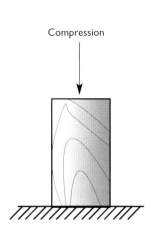

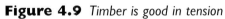
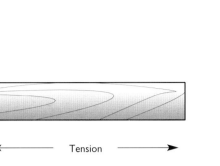

Figure 4.9 *Timber is good in tension*

Figure 4.10 *Resisting compression*

Compression and tension across the grain
Timber is weakest when a compression or tension load is applied across the grain.

Bending
Timber will bend when a load is applied to it. You can reduce the bending and increase the strength of your project by turning planks on their edge. This is shown in Figure 4.11.

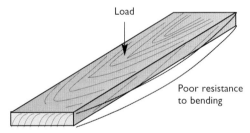

Figure 4.11 *Resisting bending forces*

Man-made boards

The term 'man-made board' is given to wood that has been cut and glued to form a board or sheet.

Advantage: One advantage of a sheet is its size. While solid timber is limited to 300 mm wide, sheets can be up to 1500 mm wide. Many of the man-made boards such as plywood can be much stronger than solid timber because of the arrangement of the grain.

Disadvantages: Prolonged exposure to moisture can often cause man-made boards such as MDF and chipboard to become weak. They are difficult to join using normal wood joints and often require special fixings. Nailing and screwing into the edge can be a problem, as the boards tend to split apart as the screw or nail goes in.

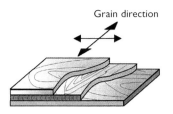

Figure 4.12 *Plywood*

Plywood

Plywood is made from layers of thin wood glued one on top of the other to form a sheet. Plywood is extremely strong and it gets this strength from the arrangement of the glued layers, which have grain directions at right angles (Figure 4.12).

MDF

MDF stands for medium density fibreboard. It is made from small particles of wood chips glued and compressed to form a sheet. While MDF is not as strong as plywood it is cheaper and very useful for making projects such as mechanical toys and boxes.

Chipboard

This is made from chips of wood compressed and glued together. It tends to be weaker than MDF and plywood. Chipboard is also a difficult material to cut, join and finish because the chips can separate when you try to screw or nail into the edges.

Timber used in technology products
Mahogany

This is an expensive, imported decorative hardwood. It is often used in those products that require a decorative finish.

Beech

This is a close-grained hardwood and is suitable for mechanical products such as children's toys, as it is non-toxic. It is also used in situations where the product is to be exposed to a lot of wear and tear.

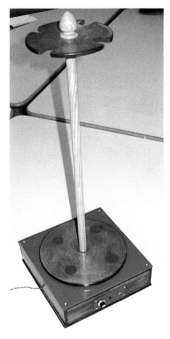

Figure 4.13 *A rotating display with its base made from mahogany*

Figure 4.14 *Beech pull-along toy frog*

Pine

There are a number of pines you can use. Most pines are inexpensive locally grown softwoods from managed forests. As they tend to be pale and have very little grain marking they are often used when appearance is not important. For example making moulds when vacuum forming. Pine has also become very popular for furniture. Figure 4.15 shows a security box made from pine designed to hold valuables.

Figure 4.15 *Pine security box*

Figure 4.16 *Cedar garden swing*

Cedar

This is a softwood that comes from North America. It is excellent for use outdoors. It contains a natural chemical that protects the timber from decay.

Manufacturing in permanent form using wood

Wood joints

Butt joint

The butt joint can be used on the corner of boxes and frames. It is the simplest of all the joints to make but it is also the weakest. The joint is simply two pieces of wood glued, butted and nailed together. A typical butt joint is shown in Figure 4.17. To improve the appearance, the nails should be punched below the surface.

Lapped joint

The lap joint is similar to the butt joint but one of the pieces has a rebate cut out for the other to fit into. The lap joint is much stronger than the butt joint because of the increased gluing surface. It is also common practice to nail the joint from both sides. A lap joint is shown in Figure 4.18.

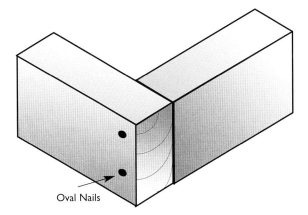

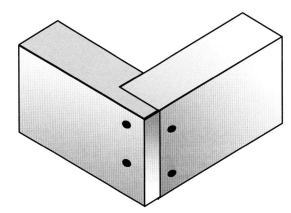

Figure 4.17 *Butt joint*

Figure 4.18 *Lapped joint*

Halving joint

The halving joint is used for making frames. As its name implies, both pieces of wood used in the joint have half their thickness removed to allow the other piece to sit down in. There are three main types of halving joint:

- 'T' halving
- cross halving
- corner halving.

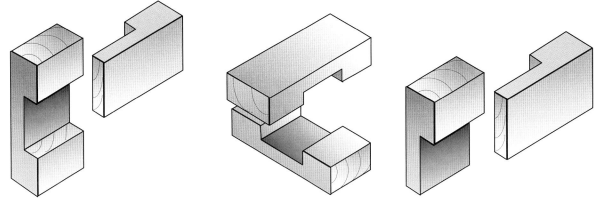

Figure 4.19 *'T' halving joint*   **Figure 4.20** *Cross halving joint*   **Figure 4.21** *Corner halving joint*

Dowel joint

Dowel joints consist of two pieces of wood jointed together with two or more round dowels. The joint is glued and cramped and left to set before the cramps are removed. Dowel joints are frequently used when making frames and joining man-made boards.

A dowel joint used on the corner of a frame is shown in Figure 4.22.

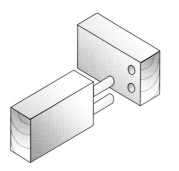

Figure 4.22 *Dowel joint*

Cramping frames and boxes

When making a frame or box, it is important to glue and cramp it correctly to ensure that all four corners are square (at 90 degrees). One method for doing this is shown in Figure 4.23. This method has four stages:

1. Apply a good quality PVA wood glue to the joints.
2. Use sash cramps to pull the joints together.
3. Make sure the diagonals are equal. If the diagonals (corner to corner) are equal the frame or box has to be square.
4. Finally, to prevent twisting make sure you leave your job on a flat level surface to dry.

Figure 4.23 *Ensuring a box has all corners at 90°*

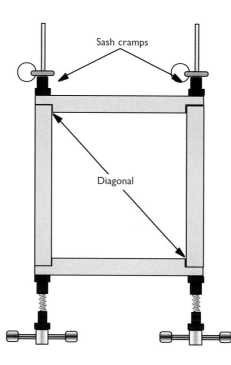

Sash cramps

Diagonal

Manufacturing using wood in semi-permanent form

Nails

Nailing is the quickest way to join two pieces of wood. Nails can be used on their own as a fixing or they can be used to cramp two pieces of wood together until the glue dries.

The three main types of nail are:

- panel pins
- oval nails
- wire nails.

The different types of nails are shown in Figure 4.24.

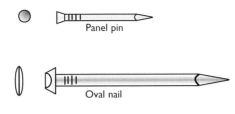

Figure 4.24 *Types of nails*

The heads of panel pins and oval nails are usually punched below the surface and the hole filled in with filler. The tool used to do this is called a **nail punch**.

Figure 4.25 *Nail punch*

Screws

Wood screws will give a strong fixing between two pieces of material as the threads pull one piece of wood against the other.

There are two main types of head used on wood screws:

- countersunk
- round-head.

Countersunk head screws are used when you want the head to be below the surface of the wood. Round-head screws are used with thin material where there is a danger of the head pulling through the material. Types of screw heads are shown in Figure 4.26.

Figure 4.26
Countersunk and round-head screws

Preparing the wood to receive a screw

It is important to prepare the wood correctly so that the screw acts as a cramping device pulling the top piece of wood down onto the bottom. To do this you should:

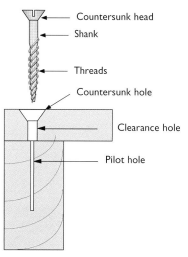

1. Drill a clearance hole in the top piece of wood just slightly larger in diameter than the shank of the screw.
2. Drill a hole, half the diameter of the shank, in the second piece of wood to act as a pilot hole for the screw. This is shown in Figure 4.27.

Figure 4.27 *Preparing the wood for countersunk screws*

Wood cutting saws

There are three main types of saws for cutting wood. These are:

- hand saws
- back saws
- coping saws.

Figure 4.28 *Wood cutting saws. Coping saw (a), hand saw (b), back saw (c).*

The saw you use will depend on the type of cut you wish to make. Some typical saws are shown in Figures 4.29 to 4.33.

Hand saws

These are used to cut large pieces of wood to size. The correct use of a hand saw is shown in Figure 4.29.

Figure 4.29 *(a) A hand saw and (b) the correct use of a hand saw*

(b)

Back saws

These are used to make accurate cuts in wood, for example when making joints. Backsaws get their name because they have a heavy strip of metal on the top edge of the blade to keep it straight during sawing. There are a number of backsaws, the most popular being the tenon saw. Figure 4.30 shows a tenon saw being used to cut a joint. Figure 4.31 shows the correct way to hold the saw.

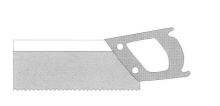

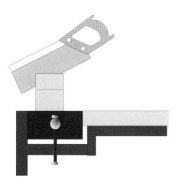

Figure 4.30 *Back saw (tenon saw)*

Figure 4.31 *Correct way to hold a back saw*

Coping saws

The coping saw was designed to cut curved shapes out of wood.

Figure 4.32 *Coping saw*

Figure 4.33 shows the correct way to hold a coping saw when cutting a curved shape.

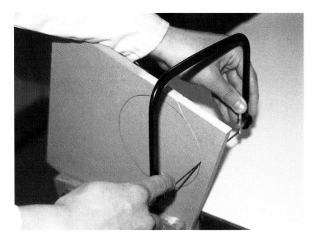

Figure 4.33 *Holding a coping saw*

Woodwork marking-out tools

The main marking-out tools are the:

- try square
- marking gauge
- steel rule.

Try square

This has a blade and handle fixed at an angle of 90° for marking and checking 90° angles. The square should be held firmly against the side of the wood while marking out.

Figure 4.34 *Using a try square*

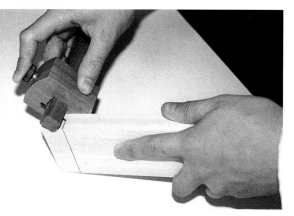

Figure 4.35 *Using a marking gauge*

Marking gauge

This is used to mark parallel lines on your wood. It has a steel pin that you use to scratch the parallel line.

Steel rule

This will be marked out in millimetres only.

Wood cutting tools

Bevel-edge chisels

These come in different widths and are used for cutting joints and general woodwork. If you need to strike the chisel, use a mallet as shown in Figure 4.36.

Smoothing plane

A smoothing plane is used either to prepare the surface of the wood for finishing after sawing or to reduce the wood in size. The correct way to use a smoothing plane is shown in Figure 4.37.

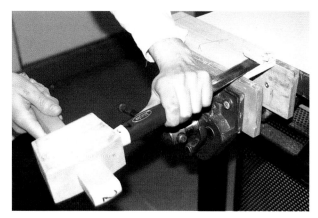

Figure 4.36 Using a bevel-edge chisel

Figure 4.37 Using a smoothing plane

59

There are a number of different metals available for you to use in your projects. These can be categorised into two main groups:

- ferrous metals
- non-ferrous metals.

Ferrous metals

The most commonly used ferrous metal is **mild steel**. Mild steel is an alloy. An alloy is a metal made by mixing two or more metals together. By doing this you can change the working properties of the metal to suit your particular needs.

Mild steel has good tensile and compressive strength. It is hardwearing and, if heated to a dull red, it can be bent and shaped easily. It can be joined by mig welding, soldering, brazing, riveting and bolting. The main disadvantage of mild steel is it will rust when exposed to the air and moisture. To prevent this you will have to treat the surface of the metal with a coating such as paint.

Non-ferrous metals

Non-ferrous metals will not rust and can be finished by cleaning and polishing. The only disadvantages are they are not as hardwearing as mild steel and they cost considerably more.

The most popular non-ferrous metals for technology projects are brass, copper and aluminium.

Brass: Easily worked, joined and very good for lathe turning. Good surface finish. Brass is an alloy made from copper and tin.

Copper: Easily worked and joined. Can be softened by annealing, then shaped with a wooden mallet. Good surface finish.

Aluminium: Easily worked but difficult to join.

Size and section of metals

Both ferrous and non-ferrous metals are available in a range of tubular sections, solid bars and sheets.

Sheet metal

Sheet metal comes in a range of sizes from 600 mm × 600 mm to 2000 mm × 1000 mm. You can buy most of the sheet sizes in a range of thicknesses from 0.6 mm to 3 mm.

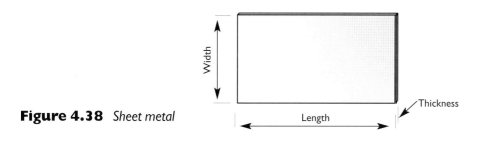

Figure 4.38 *Sheet metal*

Solid metal bar

You can buy solid bars in both ferrous and non-ferrous metals in a range of sections and sizes. The most common sections are shown in Figure 4.39.

Figure 4.39 *Solid metal bar*

Solid sections

You can buy solid section metal in both ferrous and non-ferrous metals although stockholders usually only carry these sections in mild steel. When ordering solid section of metal you must specify the sectional width and the thickness.

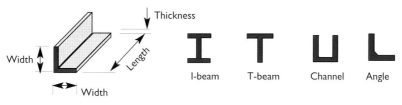

Figure 4.40 *Solid sections*

Tubular sections

You can buy both ferrous and non-ferrous metals in tubular sections (Figure 4.41).

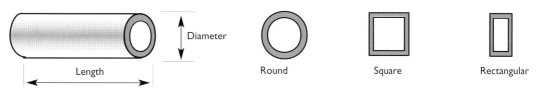

Figure 4.41 *Tubular sections*

Manufacturing metal products in permanent form

Soft soldering

Soft soldering is a quick and easy method of permanently joining two pieces metal. Copper, brass and mild steel can all be joined using soft solder, but not aluminium.

While a soft solder joint is permanent, it tends to be weak, which will limit its use.

To soft solder:

1. Clean both surfaces of the joint with emery cloth until they are free of dust and dirt (Figure 4.42).
2. Coat both cleaned surfaces of the joint with flux to keep the metal clean during soldering (Figure 4.43).
3. If necessary hold the joint together using wire to prevent movement.
4. Place the job on a heat resistant surface such as fire bricks.
5. Apply small pieces of solder along the joint.
6. Heat the two pieces of metal to approximately 230 °C using a gentle gas flame (Figure 4.44). The correct temperature is when the heated metal melts the small pieces of solder and solder starts to flow into the joint. Do not overheat the joint.

Figures 4.42 to 4.44 show two pieces of metal being soldered.

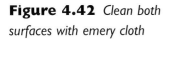

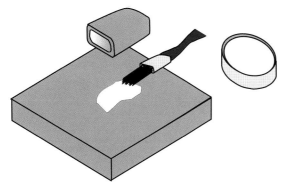

Figure 4.42 *Clean both surfaces with emery cloth*

Figure 4.43 *Apply flux to the joint*

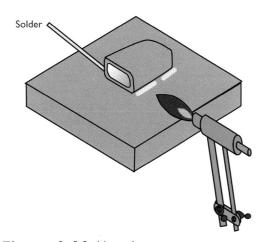

Figure 4.44 *Heat the material before applying additional solder*

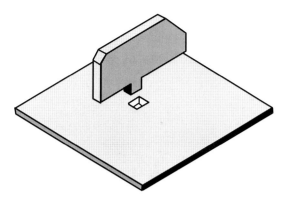

Figure 4.45 *Close fitting joint to be brazed*

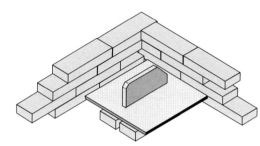

Figure 4.46 *Containing the heat*

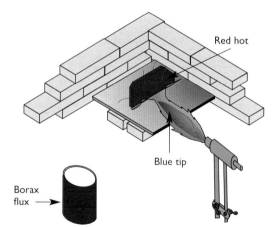

Red hot

Blue tip

Borax flux →

Figure 4.47 *Use the blue tip of the flame for greatest heat*

Brazing

Brazing provides a permanent joint in metal. Because of the high temperatures needed in this process it is mainly used for joining mild steel and is not suitable for joining copper and brass.

To braze two pieces of metal together:

1. Make a close fitting joint (Figure 4.45).
2. Clean the metal with emery cloth until it is brightly polished.
3. Place the assembled job on a heat resistant surface.
4. Heat the metal with a gas and air flame until the metal is bright red (850 °C). The correct temperature will be difficult to achieve unless you contain the heat. To do this use a brazing hearth and surround your work with firebricks (Figure 4.46). The correct flame is also important. This is one where the gas is fully on and the air is increased until the blue inner part of the flame extends three quarters of the way along the flame (Figure 4.47).
5. Dip the brazing rod into borax flux and offer it to the heated joint.
6. Keep the flame on the job but not on the joint during this stage of brazing and allow the melting rod to flow into the joint.
7. Allow the joint to cool slowly, as sudden quenching in water will cause the joint to fracture.
8. Any excess brass or flux should be cleaned off using a file or emery cloth, as excess flux will cause corrosion of the metal and prevent paint from taking to it.

Generally the brazing rod used in school workshops is a mixture of copper and zinc, which makes brass alloy. Because of the high temperatures involved it is important to wear safety glasses, leather apron and gloves while brazing.

Mig welding

Wear protec...

Mig welding provides a permanent method of joining two pieces of metal. It is generally used for welding mild steel although by using a special wire you can weld other metals such as aluminium.

To use mig welding:

1. Clamp the two pieces of metal to be joined.
2. Fix an earth clamp to your job.
3. A large current is passed along a thin steel wire. Bring the wire close to the joint so that an electric arc jumps across the joint. This arcing heats the immediate area to a high temperature causing the surface of the metal and the wire to melt and fuse together.
4. Fusing of the molten wire and the mild steel is only possible because of the flow of argon gas around the welded joint during welding. The argon shield keeps the surface clean, preventing oxidisation of the metal and allowing fusion to take place.

Figure 4.48 *Mig welder*

The temperatures involved in mig welding are lower than those associated with electric arc welding with the result that much thinner material can be welded using this process.

It is important to wear a mig welding mask during welding, as the bright arc will damage your eyesight. It is also important to wear long leather gloves and apron as hot sparks, called splatter, can jump off the job. This splatter is molten metal and will burn your clothes and skin unless you take proper precautions.

Riveting

Rivets are used to permanently join two or more pieces of metal. They are made from soft malleable metals such as soft iron, brass, copper and aluminium.

Countersunk rivets

To rivet two pieces of metal using countersunk rivets:

1. Drill a hole in both pieces of metal the same diameter as the rivet.
2. Use a countersink drill to form a countersink in both pieces of metal.
3. Cut the rivet to length. The length of the rivet should be the thickness of the metal plus the diameter of the rivet.
4. Use a ball-pein hammer to drive the rivet in and fill the countersink hole.
5. File the rivet head to remove excess metal.
6. Finish by draw filing.

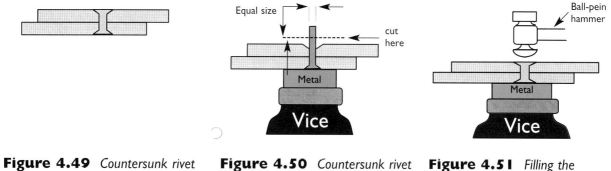

Figure 4.49 *Countersunk rivet*   **Figure 4.50** *Countersunk rivet*   **Figure 4.51** *Filling the countersunk hole*

Snap-head rivets

The technique of riveting using snap-head rivets is similar to that used with countersunk rivets. In snap-head rivets the head of the rivet is formed using the ball end of a ball-pein hammer. Two rivets sets are used to create the final shape. The technique is shown in Figure 4.53.

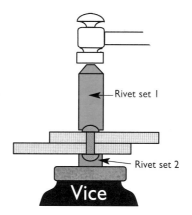

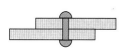

Figure 4.52 *Snap-head rivet*   **Figure 4.53** *Using rivet sets*

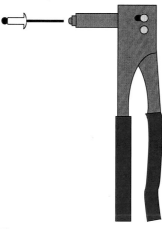

Pop riveting

Pop rivets are used to permanently join two or more pieces of sheet metal together.

The pop rivet has a hollow centre into which a hardened pin is located. The pin has a ball at one end. It is this ball that forms the second rivet head during the riveting process.

Figure 4.54 *Pop rivet tool*

To join sheet metal by pop riveting:

1. Select a rivet made from the same material as you are joining.
2. Drill a hole in both pieces of sheet material equal to the diameter of the rivet.
3. Open the jaws of the pop rivet tool and slide in the pin of the rivet.
4. Slide the rivet though the two pieces of material.
5. Squeeze the two handles together.
6. The ball at the rivet end of the pin will pull into the rivet forming the second head before the ball breaks off.

While pop riveting is quick and easy to do the mechanical joint is not very strong. The technique of pop riveting is shown in Figures 4.54 to 4.56.

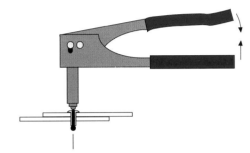

Figure 4.55 *Assembling the rivet in the material*

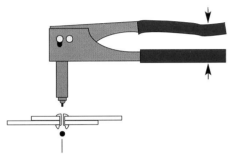

Figure 4.56 *The ball breaks off when the rivet is formed*

Manufacturing metal products in semi-permanent form

Nuts and bolts

Nuts and bolts are used to create a mechanical fixing between two pieces of metal. The most common type of nut and bolt is the hexagon-head (Figure 4.57). This enables you to tighten the nut and bolt using a spanner.

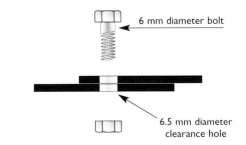

6 mm diameter bolt

6.5 mm diameter clearance hole

Figure 4.57 *Hexagon-head nut and bolt*

Washers

The purpose of a **washer** is to reduce the friction between the nut and the material being fixed.

Washer   Spring washer

Figure 4.58 *Types of washer*

A problem that can occur with nuts and bolts is that the nut can come loose as a result of vibration or friction. To overcome this problem you should use either an antifriction washer or antifriction nut or both. The most common antifriction washer is the **spring washer**. When the nut is tightened down it compresses the spring washer. It is this force that prevents the nut from working loose. Two different types of washer are shown in Figure 4.58.

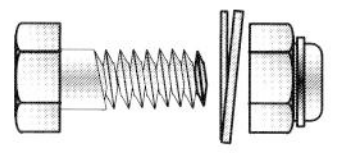

Figure 4.59 *Antifriction nut and washer*

Antifriction nuts are special nuts that are prevented from working loose by a piece of nylon added to the top of the nut. The bolt has to cut its own threads as it passes through the nut. It is this action that provides the resistance and prevents the nut from working loose. These nuts are often referred to as nylock nuts. An antifriction nut and washer are shown in Figure 4.59.

Machine screws

Machine screws are used to create a semi-permanent fixing between two or more pieces of metal. They are similar to bolts except they are tightened using a screwdriver. The three main types, which are shown in Figure 4.60, are:

- countersunk-head screw
- cheese-head screw
- round-head screw.

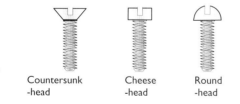

Countersunk
-head

Cheese
-head

Round
-head

Figure 4.60 *Machine screws*

Figure 4.61 *Self-tapping screw*

Self-tapping screws

These are similar to wood screws except they are made from hardened steel and the threads are cut all the way to the head of the screw. They are used to fix two pieces of sheet metal.

Metalwork fabrication

Fabrication is the term given to making products by joining pieces of metal together.

Many fabrication methods use sheet material. An example of a fabricated sheet mild steel tray and the specialist tools used to make it are shown in Figures 4.62 to 4.65.

Once the shape is marked out, use **tinsnips** to cut the profile (Figure 4.62).

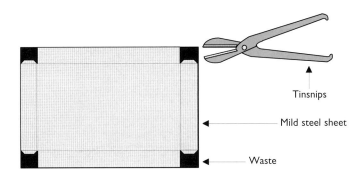

Figure 4.62 *Using tinsnips to cut the profile*

Folding bars are used to hold the sheet material and keep it straight during folding (Figure 4.63).

Holding the folding bars in the vice, place a block of hardwood on top of the side to be folded. Bend this side over to form the side of the tray (Figure 4.64).

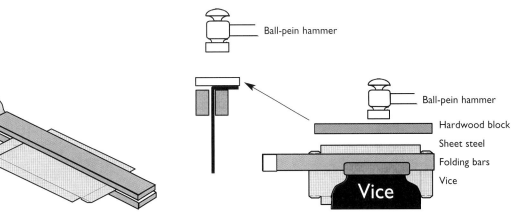

Figure 4.63 *Folding bars*

Figure 4.64 *Folding the tray*

The corners could be joined using a number of different methods. The one shown in Figure 4.65 is pop riveting. Soft soldering could also be used especially if the tray was designed to hold a liquid.

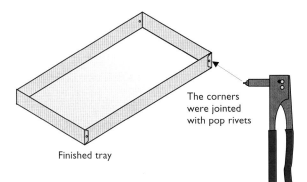

Figure 4.65 *Pop rivet joints*

Go-kart platform

Design situation

In his spare time a student was involved in racing go-karts and the kart required regular maintenance between races.

Solution

The solution was a servicing platform on which the kart would sit. The platform was designed to rise and fall quickly and safely to a height of 800 mm, saving time on servicing.

The platform jack was fabricated from tubular steel bolted together. The pivot joints had antifriction nuts and washers to prevent the nuts from working loose. Aluminium chequered plate was used on the platform. This was pop riveted to the tubular frame. A hydraulic ram was used to lift the platform to its maximum height, at which point safety pins were inserted into the joints to prevent the platform from collapsing should the ram fail. The finished project is shown in Figure 4.66.

Figure 4.66 A fabricated go-kart servicing platform

Making metalwork projects by wasting

The term 'making by wasting' means the product or part of the product is cut from a solid piece of metal. The gearwheel shown in Figure 4.67 was cut on a milling machine from a solid piece of round steel bar.

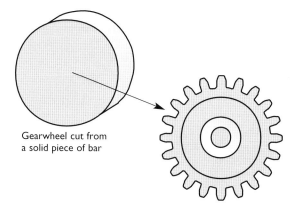

Gearwheel cut from
a solid piece of bar

Figure 4.67 *Making by wasting*

Not all wasting operations require a milling machine or centre lathe. The sliding bevel shown in Figure 4.68 was cut from flat bar.

Making a sliding bevel by wasting

The sliding bevel shown in Figure 4.68 was made from two pieces of solid bar.

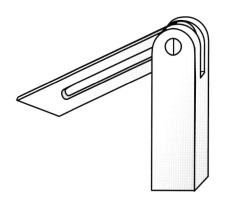

Figure 4.68 *Sliding bevel*

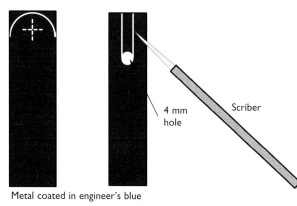

4 mm hole

Scriber

Metal coated in engineer's blue

Figure 4.69 *Marking out*

Marking out

The main body was made from 25 mm × 12 mm flat bar. This was first coated in engineer's marking blue so that the scriber lines could be easily seen (Figure 4.69).

Making the body

1. A 4 mm hole was drilled at the base of the slot while the bar was still flat and square.
2. A second-cut file was used to remove the waste material at the corners. The final shape was achieved with a smooth-cut file.

Figure 4.70 *Removing the waste by filing*

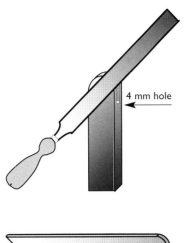

3. The waste material was removed from the slot using a hacksaw (Figure 4.72).
4. The slot was finished with a file.

Figure 4.71 *Sliding blade*

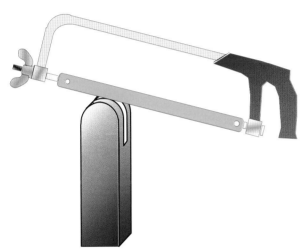

Figure 4.72 *Hacksaw to remove the waste*

Making the sliding blade

The sliding blade was made from 25 mm $\times$ 3 mm mild steel flat bar.

1. The waste material at both ends was removed with a hacksaw and second-cut file and finished with a smooth-file (Figure 4.72).
2. A series of holes was drilled along the slot using a twist drill and a drilling machine.
3. A cold chisel was used to remove the waste material between the holes. To do this the material was held firmly in the vice with the cutting line down level with the jaws of the vice. A sharp cold chisel and ball-pein hammer were used to chisel away the waste (Figure 4.73).
4. Finally the slot was filed to shape using a thin file called a warding file (Figure 4.74).

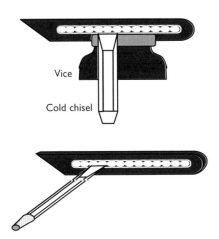

Figure 4.73 *Cutting the slot*

Figure 4.74 *Warding file*

Tapping and threading

Tapping

The term tapping refers to the process of cutting internal threads into which a screw will fit. The tool used to cut the threads is called a **tap** and it is made from high carbon steel. By holding it in a **tap wrench** you can turn the tap (Figure 4.75).

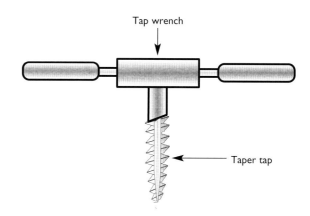

Figure 4.75 *Taper tap*

Turning the tap wrench in a clockwise direction for half a revolution cuts the threads. The tap should then be turned in reverse for half a turn to release the cuttings. This will prevent the tap from becoming clogged.

Tapping a hole in mild steel

To tap a hole you first need to drill a hole in the material just smaller than the diameter of your tap. Next apply cutting paste to the tap. Now enter the taper tap in the hole and press down to start the cut. Turn the wrench in a clockwise direction, reversing every half turn to clear the waste. This is shown in Figure 4.76.

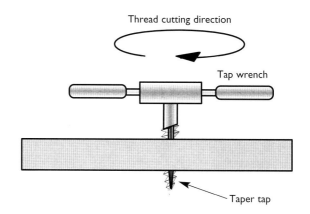

Figure 4.76 *Cutting threads using a taper tap*

Table 4.2 shows the correct size of holes you should drill when tapping.

Table 4.2 *Drill sizes*

Thread size	Tapping hole	Clearance hole
M3	2.5 mm	3.5 mm
M4	3.3 mm	4.5 mm
M5	4.2 mm	5.5 mm
M6	5.0 mm	6.5 mm
M8	6.8 mm	8.5 mm
M10	8.5 mm	10.5 mm

Threading

The term threading refers to the process of cutting external threads on the outside of a round bar. When cutting external threads a tool called a **die** is used. The die is held in a die holder. The same technique of forward and reverse cutting action is used for cutting external threads.

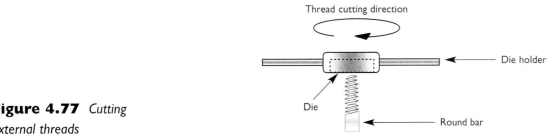

Figure 4.77 *Cutting external threads*

Portable desk lamp

Design situation

A student studying for exams works at a desk in her bedroom. The desk is in a corner away from the window. The location provides poor natural light and the nearest plug socket is across the room.

Solution

The solution was a small table lamp powered by its own 3 volt battery that was fixed along with the PCB (printed circuit board) to the underside of the shade. The final design is shown in Figure 4.78.

Stem

The final design used 8 mm diameter aluminium rod for the vertical stem and supporting arm. Both were cleaned with 00 gauge wire wool and polished on the polishing machine.

The supporting arm had external threads cut using an M8 die.

Counterweight

The counterweight was made from 30 mm aluminium rod. The rod was drilled for tapping on the centre lathe to a depth of 25 mm. Internal threads were cut using an M8 taper tap, second tap and plug tap.

Base

The base was made from beech. This is a close grain hardwood that enabled the threaded stem to cut its own threads into the wood as it was screwed in.

Plastic shade

The shade was vacuum formed over a wooden mould made from pine. It was fixed to the supporting arm with an M8 antifriction nut and washer as shown in Figure 4.79.

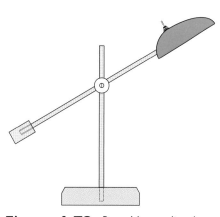

Figure 4.78 *Portable reading lamp*

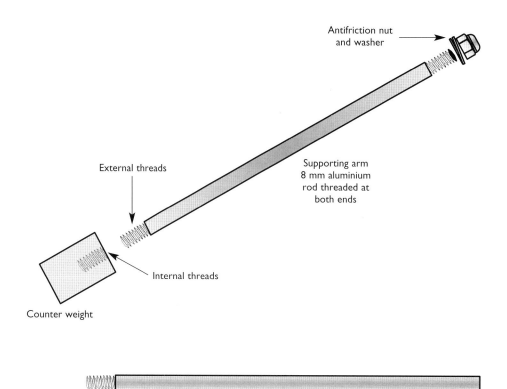

Figure 4.79 *Threaded bar*

Plastics

The three most commonly used plastics in the manufacture of technology products are:

- acrylic
- high impact polystyrene (sometimes called rigid polystyrene)
- melamine.

Plastics have the advantage over wood and metal because they have pre-finished surfaces. If care is taken not to scratch or damage these surfaces you will only need to dress and polish the edges when manufacturing plastic products.

Acrylic

This comes in sheets, tubes and solid bars. Sheets will have a protective film top and bottom to protect them against scratches. This film should be left on until the very last minute during manufacture.

If heated to 165–175 °C acrylic will become flexible, allowing you to bend and reshape it. The two most common methods of reshaping acrylic are:

- line bending
- vacuum forming.

Line bending acrylic sheet

This is a process where you heat a narrow strip along a sheet of plastic until it becomes elastic, at which point you can bend it to the required angle. A hot wire strip heater or element heater is used to heat the narrow strip on the material. Figure 4.80 shows a typical hot wire strip heater.

(a)

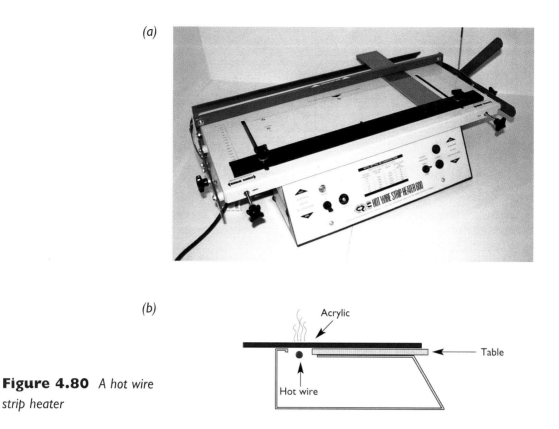

(b)

Figure 4.80 *A hot wire strip heater*

When line bending it is advisable to use a jig to hold your work in place until it cools. This will ensure the final angle is correct. The jig shown in Figure 4.81 is adjustable so that you can set the desired angle. This jig is made from wood so it will retain the heat. The trapped heat will slow down the cooling of the bend so it is good practice to have an air gap at the corner to allow the heat to escape.

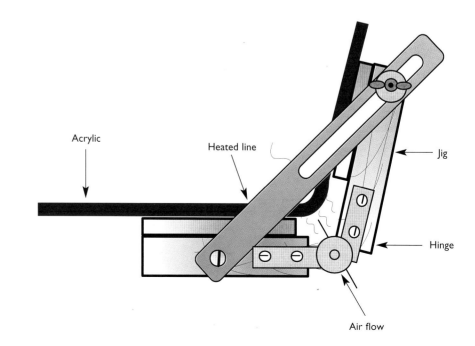

Figure 4.81 *Line bending jig*

Vacuum forming acrylic sheet

The technique used for vacuum forming acrylic sheet is similar to the technique used for vacuum forming high impact polystyrene sheet (see p.79). The only difference is that you need to pre-dry the sheet. A vacuum forming station is shown in Figure 4.82.

Figure 4.82 *Forming station*

Pre-drying acrylic sheet

If you wish to vacuum form or blow mould acrylic it is necessary to pre-dry the sheet to allow any moisture trapped in it to evaporate. If you fail to dry your sheet air bubbles will appear in the finished product as moisture turns to steam during the heating of the sheet.

To pre-dry your sheet place it in an oven for 1.25 hours per mm thickness at 40 °C

When vacuum forming or blow moulding the material must then be heated to 165–175 °C.

Blow moulding acrylic sheet

The technique of blow moulding is used to form a semi-circular dome in acrylic. The process involves pre-drying the sheet in an oven at 40 °C then increasing the temperature of the oven to 170 °C. At this temperature the sheet will become elastic. The sheet is quickly moved into a suitable blow moulding jig and air pressure applied under it. The air pressure forces the sheet up into a dome. At this point the air pressure should be reduced so that the shape is kept constant. The reduced pressure should be maintained until the sheet has cooled. Figure 4.83 shows a dome being formed using the blow moulding technique.

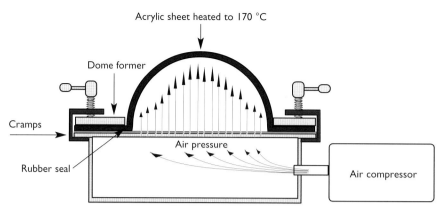

Figure 4.83 *Blow moulding machine*

Fabricating with acrylic in permanent form

Acrylic can be joined using either tensol cement or fusion cement.

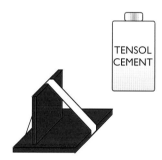

Figure 4.84 *Permanent fixing using tensol cement*

When using **tensol cement** it is good practice to pour a small amount of cement on to a piece of metal. Then dip the edge to be cemented into the liquid before locating it on the job. Finally, hold the joint secure with an elastic band or masking tape until it hardens (Figure 4.84).

Fusion cement is sometimes referred to as capillary cement because of the method of application. When using fusion cement the pieces are held in position with masking tape or a rubber band. The cement is dropped with a fine dropper needle into the corner of the joint. The cement is then drawn into the joint by capillary attraction (Figure 4.85).

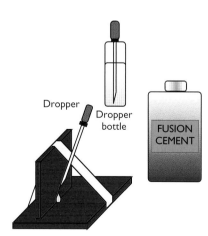

Figure 4.85 *Permanent fixing using fusion cement*

Care should be taken to avoid getting cement on any part of your job except the joint as it melts into the surface of the plastic and will permanently mark your work. Also avoid clamping your joint too tightly as this will cause crazing around the joint.

Fabricating with acrylic in semi-permanent form

If the pieces you are fabricating are to be taken apart or the material is to be used as part of a moving joint, then you can fix acrylic in the same way as you would metal. Solid bar and thick sheets can be threaded and screwed together. Or machine screws, nuts and bolts can be used to join two or more pieces of acrylic (Figure 4.86).

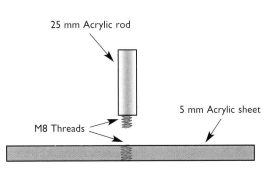

Figure 4.86 *Threading solid acrylic*

High impact polystyrene sheet

High impact polystyrene sheet is mainly used for vacuum forming. It is a pre-finished sheet that will become elastic at 90–100 °C. At this temperature it can be vacuum formed over a suitable mould. It is also possible to line bend polystyrene sheet, but care should be taken not to overheat the material. If your strip heater has a temperature control you should start by setting it at the lowest setting and increase the temperature gradually until the material becomes elastic.

Vacuum forming moulds

A mould is a temporary pattern of the final shape. The sides of the mould should be slightly tapered so that the top of your mould is smaller than the bottom (Figure 4.87). This will allow the mould to release more easily after the sheet has been vacuum formed over it. Wood is a suitable material from which to make a mould, as it is easily cut and shaped. Wooden moulds will also retain heat and allow the plastic to cool more slowly. This helps prevent stress cracks appearing in your work. To avoid excess thinning of the plastic sheet during the vacuum forming process, the height of the mould should not exceed the length or the breadth of the mould.

Mould release

While taper on the sides of your mould will help the release of the mould from the vacuum formed shape, you will also need to apply a release agent to the mould before you start to vacuum form. This will make it even easier to get the mould out of the plastic. There are a number of release agents you can buy for this job. Talcum power is also an effective release agent for wooden moulds (Figure 4.88).

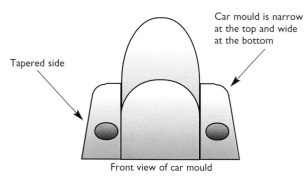

Figure 4.87 *Adding taper to the wooden mould*

Figure 4.88 *Add a release agent to the wooden mould*

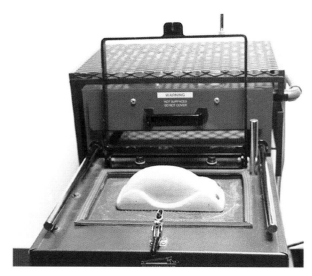

Figure 4.89 *Place the wooden mould on the vacuum forming machine*

Figure 4.90 *Wooden mould raised into soft plastic sheet*

Vacuum forming

The technique of vacuum forming requires a machine that will heat a plastic sheet before pulling the air out from below it, causing a vacuum. The soft plastic sheet will now be pulled down over a suitable mould. This process like many others, requires experience to know when the material is elastic enough and ready for forming over the mould.

The following are the stages in this process.

1. Place the wooden mould on the machine as shown in Figure 4.89.
2. The mould is lowered in the machine and the sheet fixed and clamped to the top of the machine.
3. Heat is applied to the sheet until it becomes elastic and starts to drape.
4. The heat is removed and the mould moved up into the soft plastic (Figure 4.90).
5. The vacuum is now turned on and the soft plastic will pull down over the mould.
6. Allow a few seconds for the mould to cool before turning off the vacuum.
7. Remove the sheet from the machine and pull or tap out the mould.
8. Remove the excess material. There are a number of machines available to trim plastic, one is shown in Figure 4.91.

Figure 4.91 *Trimming off the waste plastic*

Cutting and shaping plastic

Plastic can be cut and shaped in a similar way to metal, using many of the same tools.

Sawing plastic

Plastic can be cut to shape using either a hacksaw or a coping saw. Thin sheet can also be scratched with a craft knife and broken along the scratch. Figure 4.92 shows acrylic being cut with a coping saw.

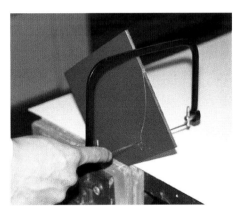

Figure 4.92 *Using a coping saw to cut acrylic*

Filing plastic

After sawing you can use metalwork files to shape and smooth your work. There is a range of different files available for this purpose. Some of these are shown in Figure 4.93.

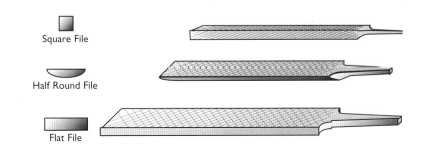

Square File

Half Round File

Flat File

Figure 4.93 *Common types of files used to shape plastics*

Finishing plastic

If you have taken care during manufacture not to damage the front and back surfaces you will only have to dress the edges. For most plastics you can finish the edges as follows:

1. Draw file the edges smooth.
2. Use a cabinet scraper to remove file marks (Figure 4.94).
3. Use wet and dry abrasive paper to remove any scratches. The abrasive paper may be wrapped around a small wooden block to keep the edge of the acrylic flat and square. This is shown in Figure 4.95.
4. Polish with acrylic polish (or Brasso) on a soft cloth (Figure 4.96).

Figure 4.94 *Hold the scraper away from you and push*

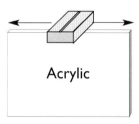

Figure 4.95 *Wet and Dry abrasive paper*

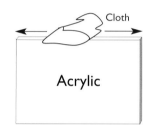

Figure 4.96 *Polish with a soft cloth*

The edges of acrylic can be polished on a **polishing machine** but care must be taken not to press too hard against the mop otherwise the acrylic will melt. The polishing machine is not suitable for dressing softer plastic such as high impact polystyrene sheet.

The correct mop is also important, so make sure the machine has a stitched mop design for plastics before you turn it on. If in doubt ask your teacher and under no circumstances should you use this machine until you have been fully trained.

Figure 4.97 *Polishing machine*

Melamine

Unlike acrylic or polystyrene melamine cannot be reshaped by heating. It is very hard wearing and is good at resisting scratching and impact. It is used in plastic products that may be exposed to high temperature. High quality kitchenware, kitchen work surfaces, cups and plates are all made from melamine. It is also used in many electrical products such as electric kettles and plug sockets.

CHAPTER FIVE   Electronics

Basic concepts

Electronics is based on the flow of electrons in a circuit. You may be wondering what electrons are. Well everything in the universe is made from atoms. These atoms consist of even smaller particles called electrons, protons and neutrons. The neutrons and protons make the centre or nucleus of the atom, while the electrons move around the nucleus, a bit like a planet and its moons. These electrons have a negative charge. The attraction between the positive nucleus and the negative electrons holds the atom together.

Figure 5.1 shows a helium atom, which has two electrons moving around its nucleus. A copper atom has 29 electrons moving around the nucleus. The electrons furthest from the nucleus are not so tightly held and so can move from atom to atom. This movement of electrons is an electric current. Some materials are better at conducting an electric current than others.

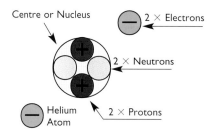

Figure 5.1 *Electrons in an atom of helium*

Conductors are materials with a structure that allows electrons to move within them with relative ease. Metals such as copper, silver, gold and aluminium are all good conductors of electrons.

Insulators are materials with a structure that doesn't allow electrons to move freely within them. Materials such as rubber and plastic make good insulators.

Semi conductors have only a few electrons free to move. Their conductivity is somewhere betweeen that of conductors and insulators. Silicone and germanium are semi conductors.

The force that makes electrons flow in a conductor is called **voltage** (symbol V) and it is measured in volts (symbol V).

An **electric current** is a flow of electrons. When we measure current (I) in a circuit we are measuring the number of electrons passing a given point in one second. Current is measured in amps, (A).

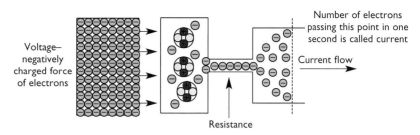

Figure 5.2 *Voltage, current and resistance*

Scientists who first studied electricity assumed that a current was a flow of *positive* charges. So in diagrams we still show current flowing in circuits from the positive to the negative side of the power supply. However, the *negatively* charged electrons are actually flowing from the negative to the positive side of the power supply. This is called 'conventional current flow'.

Resistance is a measure of how easily electrons can flow through a conductor. The greater the resistance, the more the flow of electrons is reduced. If voltage is kept constant, increasing resistance decreases the current. Resistance is measured in ohms (Ω).

Resistors

Resistance is present in a circuit when the flow of electrons is reduced. This is usually caused by a **resistor**. A resistor is a circuit component designed to reduce the flow of electrons by a specific amount. The reduction in the flow of electrons is determined by the value of the resistor. The value of a resistor is its resistance in ohms (Ω) or kilo-ohms (kΩ – often shown simply as 'k' on circuit diagrams).

The circuit symbol for a resistor is shown in Figure 5.3.

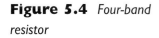

Figure 5.3 *Resistor symbol*

Types of resistor

Fixed-value resistors

There are a number of different types of fixed-value resistor which you can buy. The most commonly used is the **four-band resistor** (Figure 5.4).

Resistor values

Because resistors are so small it would be difficult to write their value on the side. Instead they have colour bands. The first two bands represent numbers, the third the number of zeros and the fourth the tolerance or accuracy of the resistor.

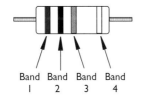

Figure 5.4 *Four-band resistor*

Band 1 Band 2 Band 3 Band 4

Table 5.1 can be used to find the value of a resistor.

Table 5.1 *Resistor values*

Colour of the band	Band 1 1st digit	Band 2 2nd digit	Band 3 *Number of zeros after the 2nd digit*	Band 4 Tolerance
Black	0	0	–	
Brown	1	1	0	
Red	2	2	00	1%
Orange	3	3	000	2%
Yellow	4	4	0000	
Green	5	5	00000	
Blue	6	6	000000	
Violet	7	7	0000000	
Grey	8	8	00000000	
White	9	9	000000000	
Gold				5%
Silver				10%

Example

To find the value of the resistor shown in Figure 5.4 you would consult Table 5.1.

1st band: red = 2
2nd band: black = 0
3rd band: orange = 000 (3 zeros)
4th band: gold = 5%

So the value of the resistor in Figure 5.4 is 20 000 ohms or 20k (5% tolerance).

Variable resistors

A variable resistor can be adjusted to alter its resistance. A preset variable resistor is set to the desired value and then left at that setting. The symbol for a variable resistor is shown in Figure 5.5.

Figure 5.5 *Symbol for a variable resistor*

Light dependent resistors (LDRs)

These are semiconductor devices whose resistance decreases when light shines on them. They are useful in light-sensing circuits. The symbol for an LDR is shown in Figure 5.6.

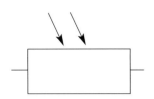

Figure 5.6 *Symbol for an LDR*

Calculating the resistance of more than one resistor

Resistors in series

The total resistance of resistors in series (as in Figure 5.7) can be found by using the following formula:

$$R_{total} = R_1 + R_2$$

Find the total resistance of the two resistors in Figure 5.7.

$$R_{total} = 1k + 1k$$
$$= 2k$$

Figure 5.7 *Resistors in series*

Resistors in parallel

The total resistance for resistors in parallel (as in Figure 5.8) can be calculated by using the following formula:

$$\frac{1}{R_{total}} = \frac{1}{R_1} + \frac{1}{R_2}$$

Find the total resistance of two resistors in parallel.

$$\frac{1}{R_{total}} = \frac{1}{2k} + \frac{1}{3k}$$

$$\frac{1}{R_{total}} = \frac{3 + 2}{6}$$

$$\frac{1}{R_{total}} = \frac{5}{6}$$

$$R_{total} = \frac{6}{5} = 1.2k$$

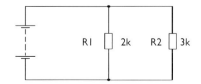

Figure 5.8 *Resistors in parallel*

Switches turn a circuit on or off by making or breaking a connection.

Types of switches

Push switches

These are switches that make or break the connection when they are pressed. There are two main types:

- push-to-make
- push-to-break.

The symbols for these are shown in Figure 5.9.

Toggle switches

Toggle switches have a lever that is thrown to make or break the connections. The example shown in Figure 5.10 is a single pole single throw (SPST) switch.

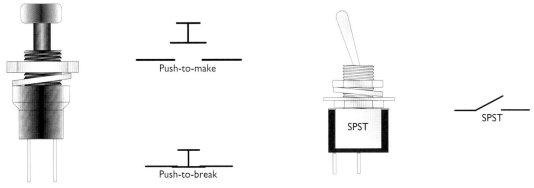

Push-to-make

Push-to-break

Figure 5.9 *Push switch and symbol*

SPST

SPST

Figure 5.10 *Toggle switch and symbol*

Micro-switches

Micro-switches are designed for situations where the connection has to be broken by a moving object. The switch has a common contact (COM), one contact that is normally closed (NC) and one that is normally open (NO). When the contacts are arranged in this way they are called single pole double throw switches (SPDT). A SPDT switch is shown in Figure 5.11.

Slide switches

Double pole double throw switches (DPDT) are used to switch on and off two or more circuits simultaneously. They are often used in motor reversing circuits (Figure 5.12).

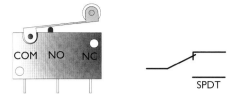

Figure 5.11 *Micro-switch and symbol*

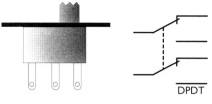

Figure 5.12 *Slide switch and symbol*

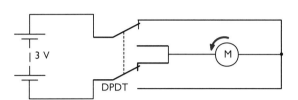

Figure 5.13 *Anti-clockwise rotation*

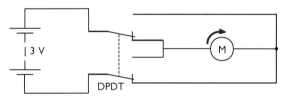

Figure 5.14 *Clockwise rotation*

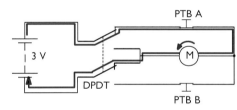

Figure 5.15 *Limit switches*

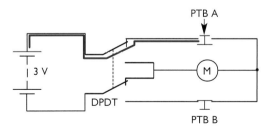

Figure 5.16 *Cutting the power*

Reversing circuit for a motor

Anti-clockwise rotation

You can use a double pole double throw switch to reverse the rotation of a d.c. motor. The circuit in Figure 5.13 uses a DPDT slide switch to change the **polarity** at the motor, that is, which side of the motor is connected to the positive terminal of the battery. When the positive supply comes in at the right- hand side of the motor it rotates in an anti-clockwise direction.

Clockwise rotation

When the switch is changed as shown in Figure 5.14 the positive supply arrives at the left-hand side of the motor, causing it to rotate clockwise.

Adding limit switches

The circuit shown in Figures 5.13 and 5.14 will run continuously. If you were using this circuit to open a window it would be important to have the motor stopping when the window was fully open or closed. To achieve this you would need push-to-break limit switches. Figure 5.15 shows the position of the limit switches in the circuit.

When the power is turned on the motor turns anti-clockwise until it reaches its limit and pushes open a limit switch. This cuts the power to the motor as shown in Figure 5.16.

Only when the DPDT switch is changed over will the power flow in the bottom half of the circuit enabling the motor to turn clockwise. It will continue to turn until the bottom limit switch is pressed, at which point the power will be cut to the motor.

Transistors

Transistors are semiconductor devices. This means that they have a resistance to the flow of electrons (current). However, they become conductors when a small voltage is present at one of the legs, called the base leg.

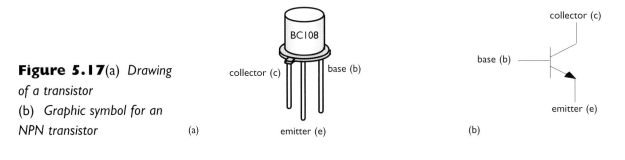

Figure 5.17(a) *Drawing of a transistor*
(b) *Graphic symbol for an NPN transistor*

You can use the transistor as a high-speed switch. If a small voltage of 0.6–1.6 V is applied to the base leg it will at once enable a larger current to flow through the transistor from the collector to the emitter. A typical transistor circuit is shown in Figure 5.18, which is an automatic light-sensing circuit.

During the day the resistance of the LDR is low so most of the current flows through this part of the circuit and the voltage at the base leg of the transistor is only 0.59 V. This is less than the 0.6 V required to turn it on, therefore the bulb remains off.

In darkness the resistance of the LDR will increase, forcing more electrons down to the base of the transistor.

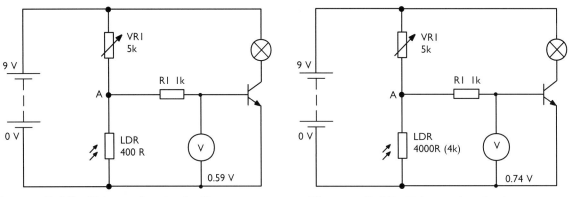

Figure 5.18 *Light-sensing circuit off*

Figure 5.19 *Light-sensing circuit on*

In Figure 5.19 the voltage has reached 0.74 V and the transistor is on. When the transistor is on current can flow in the outer part of the circuit, switching on the bulb.

Capitals

Capacitors are electronic devices that can be used to give a time delay in a circuit.

They have the ability to store a quantity of electrons, called the charge, and in some ways are like a small rechargeable battery in that they can be charged and then release this charge. The main difference is the amount of charge (electrons) they can store and the release rate. Batteries will release their charge over a long period of time, whereas capacitors release their charge almost instantly.

Capacitor values

The value of a capacitor is expressed in farads (F). A 1 farad capacitor would be the size of an aluminium soft drink can, just a little too large to use in your electronic circuits. The value of a capacitor is usually less than 1 F. Table 5.2 shows the common units used when working with capacitors.

Table 5.2 *Capacitor units*

farad	F	I	
millifarad	mF	1000	$\times 10^{-3}$
microfarad	μF	1000 000	$\times 10^{-6}$
nanofarad	nF	1 000 000 000	$\times 10^{-9}$
picofarad	pF	1 000 000 000 000	$\times 10^{-12}$

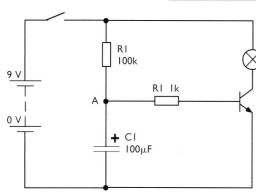

Figure 5.20 *Timer circuit off*

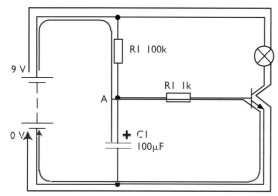

Figure 5.21 *Timer circuit on*

Capacitors in circuits

The diagrams in Figures 5.20 and 5.21 are of a timer circuit that uses a capacitor to give a small time delay before the lamp comes on.

When the circuit is turned on, the electrons flow through the left-hand loop of the circuit to fill the capacitor. When the capacitor is full the electrons must flow from A through R1 to the base of the transistor (red line in Figure 5.21). This switches the transistor on so that a current flows through the lamp (blue line) and the lamp is illuminated. The time it takes to fill the capacitor will depend on the value of R1 × C1.

The problem with this type of circuit is the time delay you are likely to get. Time delays of more than a few minutes are impractical because large capacitors have poor tolerances.

Figure 5.22 *Axial electrolytic capacitor*

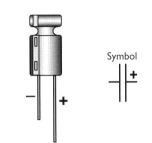

Symbol

Figure 5.23 *Radial electrolytic capacitor*

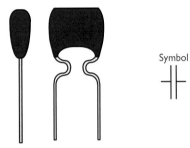

Symbol

Figure 5.24 *Metallised polyester capacitor*

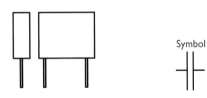

Symbol

Figure 5.25 *Miniature polyester capacitor*

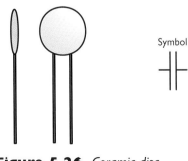

Symbol

Figure 5.26 *Ceramic disc capacitor*

An electrolytic capacitor over 1000 µF will allow charge to leak through it. This will prevent it from providing enough overflow electrons to turn on the transistor.

Types of capacitors

There are a number of different types of capacitors you can use in your circuit. The choice will depend on the value and the accuracy required.

Electrolytic capacitors

There are two main types of electrolytic capacitor, axial and radial. These are polarised capacitors and must be connected the correct way round.

These are large value capacitors and are used for long time delays or as smoothing capacitors in circuits.

Typical value range: 1 µF – 4700 µF
Tolerance: ±20%

Metallised polyester capacitor

These are non-polarised, which means they may be connected either way round. They tend to have a higher degree of tolerance and accuracy than the electrolytic capacitors.

Medium value capacitors.

Typical value range: 10 nF – 470 nF
Tolerance: ±10 – 20%

Miniature polyester capacitors

Typical value range: 1 nF–1 µF
Tolerance: ±10%

Ceramic disc capacitor

These are non-polarised, so may be connected either way round.

Up to 4.7 nF they tend to have a higher degree of tolerance and accuracy than both polyester and electrolytic capacitors.

Typical value range: 100 pF – 4.7 nF
Tolerance: ±10%

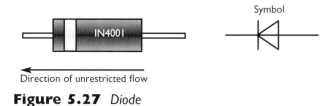

Direction of unrestricted flow

Figure 5.27 *Diode*

Symbol

Diodes

Diodes are semi-conductors that allow electrons to flow through them in one direction only.

LEDs

LED stands for Light Emitting Diode. An LED gives off light when current flows through it in one direction. LEDs are often used in electronic products in place of bulbs as they consume much less power. They are often used in hi-fi systems as stand-by indicator lights. An LED and its symbol is shown in Figure 5.28.

Figure 5.28 *An LED and its symbol*

The drawing in Figure 5.29 shows an LED. The LED must be connected the correct way round to prevent it being damaged. The leg nearest the small flat on the rim must be connected to the negative supply.

It is necessary to protect LEDs from too much current. If any type of battery other than a button cell is to be used then you must put a resistor in series with the LED. The following are suggested resistor values for different voltages.

$$3 \text{ V} - 120 \text{ } \Omega$$
$$5 \text{ V} - 220 \text{ } \Omega$$
$$9 \text{ V} - 470 \text{ } \Omega$$
$$12 \text{ V} - 560 \text{ } \Omega$$

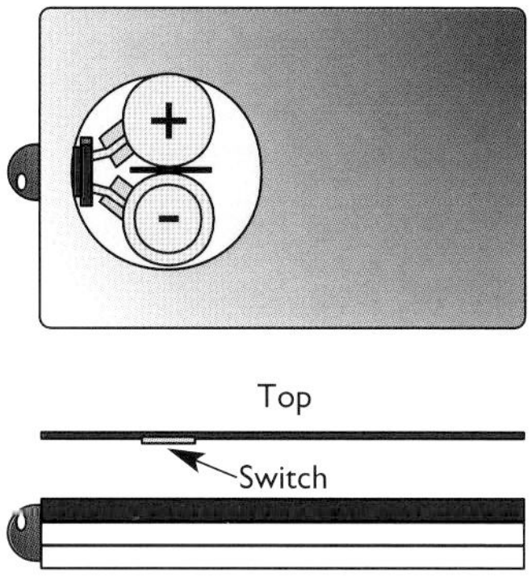

Figure 5.29 *Key Fob Torch which uses an LED as the light source*

Figure 5.30 shows a 5 mm LED used in a key fob torch. The two 1.2 volt button cell batteries are connected in series to give a total voltage of 2.4 volts. Small button cell batteries like this can be used with LEDs without a current limiting resistor as they only give out a small current that will not damage the LED.

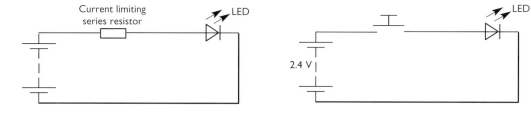

Figure 5.30 *Current limiting resistor*

Types of LEDs

The most popular LED is the 5 mm round. You can also buy 3 mm round. Less popular but still very useful are the rectangular, triangular and square LEDs. All types of LEDs mentioned can be bought in a range of colours.

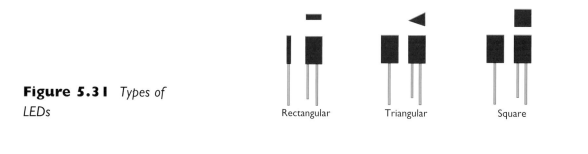

Figure 5.31 *Types of LEDs*

Torch circuit

How it works

When the push-to-make switch is pressed the electrons flow out of the battery through the protective resistor to the LED. As they pass through the LED they make it glow and you see this as light. The circuit was made using a PCB.

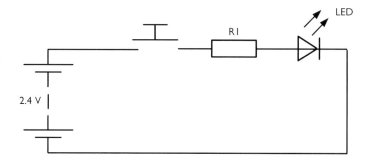

Figure 5.32 *LED circuit*

PCBs

PCB stands for Printed Circuit Board. This is a plastic board with a copper layer on one or both sides. Circuits in this book will be made on boards with copper on one side only (single sided).

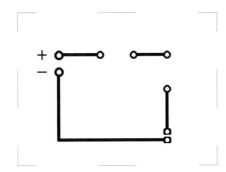

Figure 5.33 *PCB artwork*

Making a PCB

To make a PCB you must remove most of the copper, leaving a strip that will become the conductor between components on your board. This is achieved by making a suitable artwork to place on top of a copper board coated with photographic film. The film is exposed to ultraviolet light. Areas of the film unprotected by the dark lines on your artwork become unstable. The board is then placed in a developing solution for a short period of time to remove the unstable areas of film. You are now left with a developed board that is ready for etching. Etching is the term given to the process of placing the developed board in a tank containing a chemical heated to 40 °C. The chemical dissolves any unprotected copper, leaving you with a PCB that has a copper track on one side. Holes are now drilled in the copper track and the components passed through from the topside. The components are permanently fixed to the copper track by soldering.

Silk screen

This is a drawing showing where the components are placed on the PCB. It will also give the value of each component.

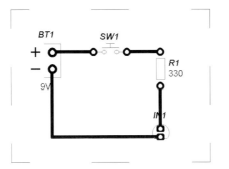

Figure 5.34 *Silkscreen view of the PCB*

Top view of the board

This is what you will see when you look at the top of the finished PCB.

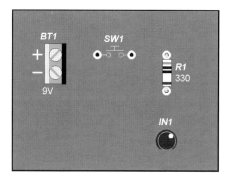

Figure 5.35 *Top view of the board*

Note: If you plan to use button cell batteries it is not necessary to use a current-limiting resistor.

Light-Sensing Circuits

Electronic circuits can be made to come on or off when the light level falls. The most common sensor used in these circuits is the LDR (light dependent resistor).

Night light

Figure 5.36 *Automatic night light*

Design situation

Young children are often frightened of the dark. There is a need for a small battery operated light which will come on automatically when it becomes dark.

Solution

The final solution this student designed was the toadstool shaped night-light shown in Figure 5.36.

How it works

The LDR sensor at the base of the lamp detects the light level. When it is dark a small bulb under the dome comes on. The bulb will stay on until it is light again.

The circuit

The circuit is powered by a 9 volt PP3 battery. When the on/off switch (SW1) is closed power goes to the circuit.

The LDR (light dependent resistor) is the sensor and its resistance increases with darkness. The variable resistor allows you to set how dark it will be before the lamp comes on.

The transistor is a high-speed switch that turns on when a voltage of 0.6–1.6 V is present at its base leg b.

The lamp will only come on if the transistor is on. The bulb must have at least 10 ohms resistance for this circuit to work.

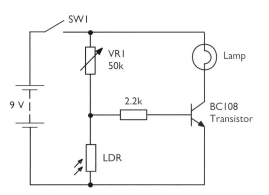

Figure 5.37 *Night-light circuit*

Block diagram for the night-light

Circuits can be divided into three main building blocks. These are **input**, **process** and **output**.

The automatic light circuit can be divided into these three main building blocks:

Input: LDR with its variable resistor. This is the sensor part of the circuit
Process: Transistor with its protective resistor
Output: Lamp

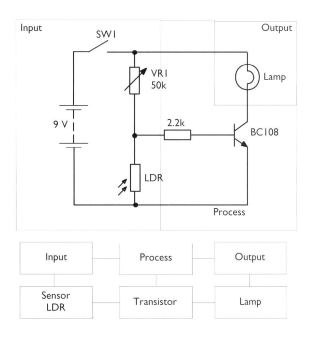

Figure 5.38 *Block diagram for light sensitive circuit*

How the dark-activated circuit works

When you close the on/off switch during the day, current flows from the battery down through the variable resistor to the LDR (red line in Figure 5.39). As light is falling on the LDR it will have a very low resistance and act as a conductor. Current flows through it back to the battery.

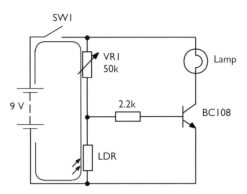

Figure 5.39 *Path of current during the day*

In the dark the LDR will have a very high resistance. This means the current cannot pass through it and must find another route back to the battery. It goes to the transistor, which acts as a high-speed electronic switch (Figure 5.40).

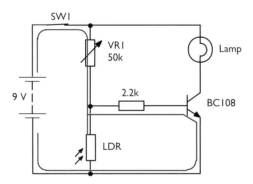

Figure 5.40 *Path of current at night*

As the transistor switches on, electrons flow around the output part of the circuit (blue line in Figure 5.41). Electrons flowing through the filament of the bulb make it glow white-hot. In this process there will be four energy changes:

- chemical energy
- electrical energy
- heat energy
- light energy.

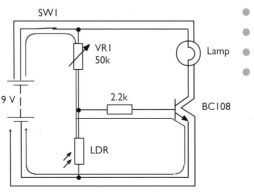

Figure 5.41 *Path of the current through the output part of the circuit (blue)*

How the light-activated circuit works

This circuit works the opposite way to the dark-activated circuit in that it is designed to come on when light falls on the LDR. An automatic daylight circuit could be used in a security box.

In this circuit the LDR would be above VR1. This is shown in Figure 5.42.

When the switch is in the on position the alarm would sound if the box was opened, allowing light to shine on the LDR.

If it is dark the LDR will have a high resistance. In this state the current cannot pass through it. The circuit remains off (green line in Figure 5.42).

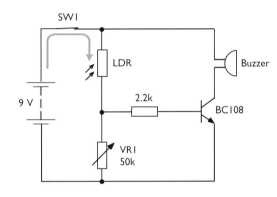

Figure 5.42 *Path of current when the circuit is in darkness*

When light falls on the LDR it becomes a conductor, so that current flows to turn on the transistor. When the transistor is on the current can pass through it and return to the battery. As the transistor is now on (red line), the electrons can now flow through the output part of the circuit (blue line). When this happens, the buzzer will come on (Figure 5.43).

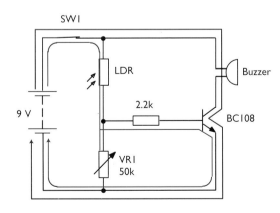

Figure 5.43 *Path of the current when the circuit is in light*

Notes on the dark-activated circuit night light

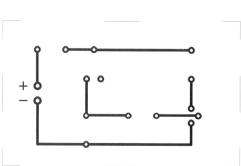

Figure 5.44 *PCB mask for dark-activated circuit*

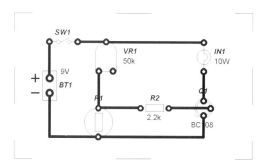

Figure 5.45 *Silk screen for dark-activated circuit*

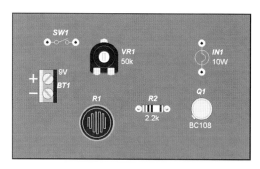

Figure 5.46 *Top view of the PCB for dark-activated circuit*

LDR

The LDR worked well as a sensor but would only respond to large changes in light levels.

Variable Resistor

Values of 22k – 47k worked well.

Transistor

The BC108 transistor was used as a simple high-speed electronic switch. Problems occurred with the BC108 when the output was changed to one requiring a flow of current larger than 300 mA (e.g. an electric motor). This caused the transistor to overheat and shortened its life span. If you wish to drive this type of output the BFY51 was slightly better but there was a marked drop in sensitivity.

Bulb

The choice of bulb was very important. It was found that most low cost bulbs had an internal resistance of 1–3 ohms. This is too low. Try to purchase bulbs with a resistance of 9–11 ohms. Low value bulbs cause the transistor to overheat and burn out.

Power supply

The battery had a life of only a few days if left on all the time. A better solution was a sealed power supply with a matching jack plug socket. This replaced the battery. Most pupils had a sealed power supply at home as part of an electronic game and were able to use these with their project.

Components

1 × 2.2k resistor
1 × 50k horizontal miniature preset (variable resistor)
1 × 9 V battery connector
1 × BC108 transistor
1 × board (76.2 mm × 55.9 mm)
1 × ORP12 LDR
1 × 6 V bulb
1 × bulb holder

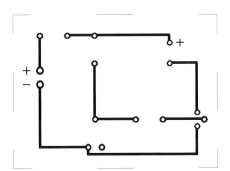

Figure 5.47 *PCB mask for light-activated circuit*

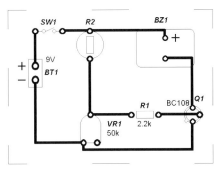

Figure 5.48 *Silk screen for light-activated circuit*

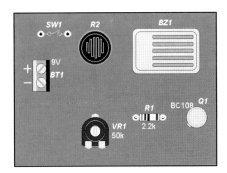

Figure 5.49 *Top view of the PCB for light-activated circuit*

LDR

When the LDR was placed in the top part of the circuit it worked well as a sensor, but as with the night light would only respond to large changes in light levels.

Variable resistor

It was found that the value of VR1 had to be increased to 100k.

Buzzer

It was found that most of the low cost 6 volt buzzers work fine.

Key switch

SW1 was changed to a low cost key switch. These were easily obtained from most of the major suppliers.

Transistor

The BC108 transistor was used as a simple high-speed electronic switch. As the alarm tended to be on for short periods there was no real problem with the BC108.

Power supply

It was found that when the circuit was in a waiting state, it consumed very little power from the battery. Unlike the night light circuit this battery lasted a long time and there was no real need for a separate power supply.

Components

1 × 2.2k resistor
1 × 100k horizontal miniature preset (variable resistor)
1 × 9 V battery connector
1 × BC108 transistor
1 × Board (76.2 mm × 55.9 mm)
1 × ORP12 LDR
1 × 6 V buzzer

Latched Alarm Circuit

Electronic circuits can be designed so that they will sound an alarm. The alarm can be made to stay on until you reset it. This is called latching the circuit.

Example **Burglar alarm**

Design situation

Homes are at constant risk from burglars. Many of these burglaries happen during the night while the people who live in the house are in bed. There is a need for a small individual alarm which could be fixed to a bedroom door.

Solution

The final solution was a latched alarm that was turned on/off by using a personal key switch (Figure 5.50).

How it works

The box is fixed to the door frame and the key switch is turned on. If the door is opened the alarm inside the box will sound. It is the key holder who resets the alarm.

The door sensor is a magnetic reed switch. The reed switch is fixed to the side of the box and the magnet is fixed to the edge of the door.

Figure 5.50 *The latched door alarm*

Circuit diagram

The circuit is powered by means of a PP3 9 V battery. When the on/off key switch is closed power goes to the circuit.

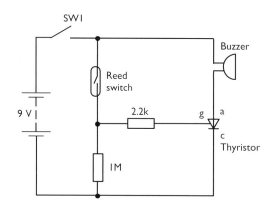

Figure 5.51 *Latched alarm circuit*

A **reed switch** was used as the sensor. This is a switch that has two fine wires that come together when a magnet is placed close to them.

The **thyristor** is a latching device. It comes on when a small voltage is present at the gate leg (g). It can only be turned off again by cutting the power to the anode leg (a). The buzzer will sound when the thyristor is on.

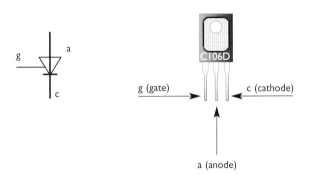

g

a

c

g (gate)

c (cathode)

C106D

a (anode)

Figure 5.52 *A thyristor and its symbol*

Block diagram

Circuits can be divided into three main building blocks. These are input, process and output.

Input: Reed switch. This is the sensor part of the circuit
Process: Thyristor with its protective resistor
Output: Buzzer

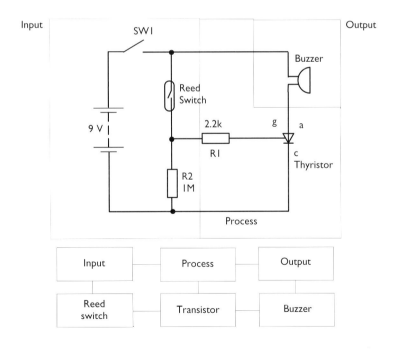

Figure 5.53 *Block diagram for the latched alarm circuit*

How it works

When the key switch (SW1) is turned to the on position the alarm is set. The current cannot flow past the open reed switch (Figure 5.54).

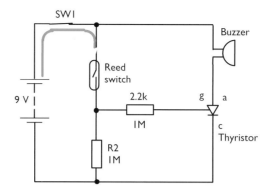

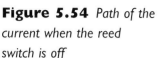

Figure 5.54 *Path of the current when the reed switch is off*

The alarm is activated by an intruder when the magnet on the door moves past the reed switch as the door is opened. When this happens the fine wires inside the reed switch close.

At this point the current will flow down to the gate leg of the thyristor (g) and cause it to switch on. Figure 5.55 shows the path of the current through the thyristor. The electrons are now able to return to the battery.

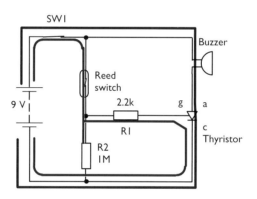

Figure 5.55 *Path of the current when the reed switch is closed*

The thyristor is a latching device. That means, once it is on it will stay on, until you turn it off. To turn off the thyristor you must cut the power to its anode leg (a). You can do this by opening the key switch (SW1).

When the thyristor is on current can flow through the output loop of the circuit making the buzzer vibrate and giving out sound.

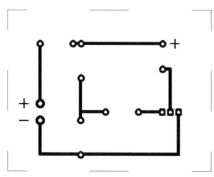

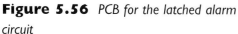

Figure 5.56 *PCB for the latched alarm circuit*

Notes on the latched alarm circuit
Reed switch: SW1

The standard proximity switch used in commercial house alarms worked well as the sensor. These are available from most electronic suppliers and come as a set. The permanent magnet fits into a 9 mm hole drilled in the edge of the door while the reed switch is enclosed in a plastic housing with flying leads.

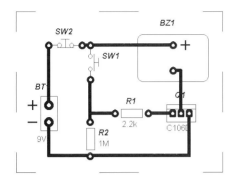

Figure 5.57 *Silk screen for the latched alarm circuit*

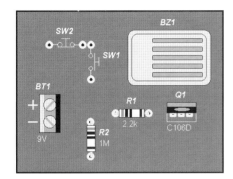

Figure 5.58 *Top view of the latched alarm PCB*

Buzzer: BZ1

Problems were experienced with buzzers that pulsed as these would cut off the power to the anode side of the thyristor. When this happened the thyristor would reset, effectively cancelling the alarm.

PCB-mounted buzzers were found to be more secure in the casing.

Switch: SW2

A low cost circular key switch was used and this was found to be a good choice as the key could be removed after setting the alarm.

Thyristor: C106D

A C106D was used but care should be exercised when handling and soldering, as certain types are sensitive to static.

Power supply: PP3 battery

It was found that when the circuit was in a waiting state, it consumed very little power from the battery.

Components

1 × 1M resistor
1 × 2.2k resistor
1 × 9 V battery connector
1 × C106D thyristor
1 × board (73.6 mm × 55.9 mm)
1 × PCB-mounted buzzer
1 × proximity switch (compact set in a plastic housing)

Temperature Sensing Circuit

Electronic circuits can be designed so that they will detect changes in temperature and then activate an alarm.

Example

Frost alarm

Design situation

During the winter freezing temperatures can cause problems for the old or infirm. Problems can arise when a room becomes too cold for living in. There is a need for a warning device that would sound an alarm or a flashing light when the temperature falls below the recommended level.

Solution

The final solution was a plastic box with a drawing of a person dressed for the cold (Figure 5.59).

Figure 5.59 *Drawing of the frost alarm*

How it works

The black sensor on the sleeve of the coat is a thermistor. This is a sensor that detects changes in temperature. If the temperature falls too low, the circuit sounds an alarm.

The circuit has a manual switch so that the alarm can be turned off. The thermistor (sensor) comes out through the case so that it can detect the room temperature.

Circuit diagram

The circuit is powered by means of a PP3 9 volt battery. When the on/off switch is closed power goes to the circuit. The temperature sensor is a **thermistor**. This is a type of variable resistor whose resistance increases as it becomes cold. When this happens the current flows to turn on the transistor. When the transistor is on the buzzer will be on. The variable resistor allows you to set the sensitivity of the circuit.

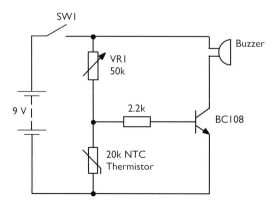

Figure 5.60

Temperature sensing circuit

Block diagram

The moisture sensing circuit can be divided into these three main building blocks.

Input: Thermistor. This is the sensor for the circuit
Process: Transistor with its protective resistor
Output: Buzzer

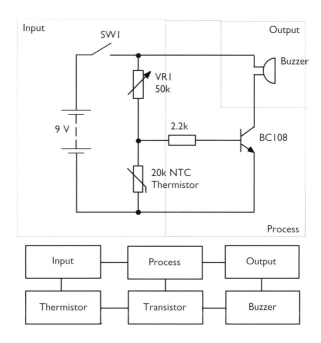

Figure 5.61 *Block diagram for the temperature sensing circuit*

Notes on the temperature sensing circuit frost alarm

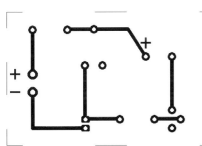

Figure 5.62 *PCB for the temperature sensing circuit*

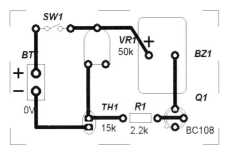

Figure 5.63 *Silk screen for the temperature sensing circuit*

Sensor thermistor

There are a number of thermistors available in most good catalogues. NTC (negative temperature coefficient) thermistors are the most common and decrease their resistance with heat. If a 20k thermistor at 25 °C is used, it will work fine with the 50k variable resistor above it.

Variable resistor

VR1 was a 50k miniature preset.

Buzzer

It was found that most of the low cost 6 volt buzzers work fine but the PCB-mounted type was found to be more secure in the casing.

Switch

SW1 was a SPST toggle switch

Transistor

The BC108 transistor was used as a simple high-speed electronic switch. As the buzzer tended to be on only for short periods there were no real problems with the BC108.

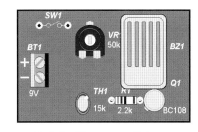

Figure 5.64 *Top view of the temperature sensing PCB*

Power supply

It was found that when the circuit was in a waiting state it consumed a lot of power from the battery. A small external power supply connected by means of a jack plug socket solved this problem.

Components

1 × 100k horizontal miniature preset
1 × 2.2k resistor
1 × 9 V battery connector
1 × BC108 transistor
1 × board (61 mm × 38 mm)
1 × PCB-mounted buzzer
1 × 20k disc NTC thermistor

Moisture Sensing Circuit

Electronic circuits can be designed so that they will detect moisture and sound an alarm.

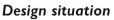

Bath level indicator

Design situation

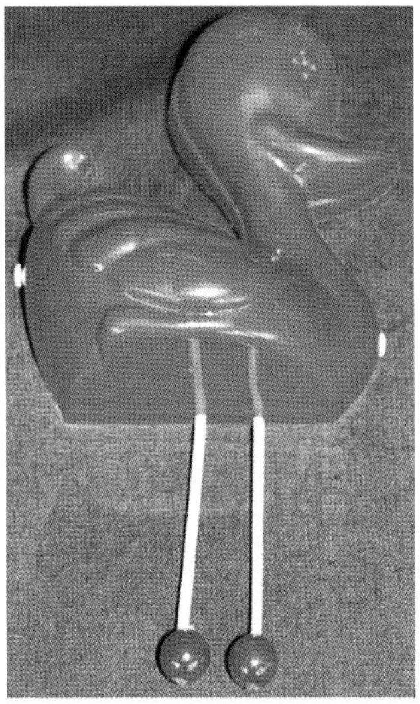

A mother running the bath for her baby found it took a long time to fill. During this time she had to stay in the bathroom and wait until the water had reached the required level. This meant a lot of time wasted while the bath filled. There is a need for a warning device that would let her know when the bath water was at the correct level.

Solution

The final solution was in the shape of a vacuum formed plastic duck with two moisture probes in the feet. The duck was fixed to the bath at the correct height using double-sided tape (Figure 5.65).

How it works

The two legs of the duck are metal probes. When the water in the bath reaches these a buzzer sounds inside the duck.

Figure 5.65 *Picture of the bath level indicator*

Circuit diagram

The circuit is powered by means of a PP3 9 volt battery. When the on/off switch is closed power goes to the circuit. The moisture sensors are two metal probes set 25 mm apart. When these are put in water the water acts as a conductor and current flows between them. When this happens a small amount of current also flows down to the base leg of the transistor, turning it on. The buzzer will sound when the transistor is on. The variable resistor allows you to set the sensitivity of the probes.

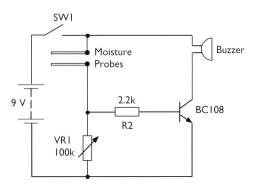

Figure 5.66 *Moisture sensing circuit*

Block diagram

Circuits can be divided into three main building blocks. These are input, process and output.

Input: Moisture probes with its variable resistor. This is the sensor part of the circuit
Process: Transistor with its protective resistor
Output: Buzzer

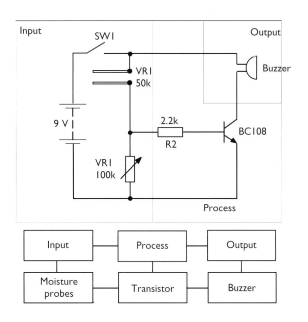

Figure 5.67 *Block diagram for the moisture sensing circuit*

Notes on the moisture sensing circuit bath level indicator

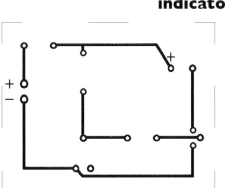

Figure 5.68 *PCB for the moisture sensing circuit*

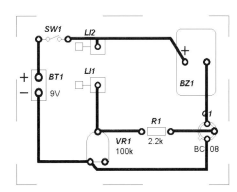

Figure 5.69 *Silk screen for the moisture sensing circuit*

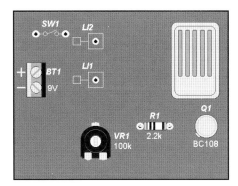

Figure 5.70 *Top view of the PCB*

Probes

These were made from 3 mm brass rod threaded at the end. Heat shrink cable was used to insulate the probes, leaving only that part of the rod that passed through the balls to act as conductors. Solder tags were used to secure the wires from the PCB to the probes. When the probes were placed in the top part of the circuit they worked well as sensors. The probes were held to the casing with 3 mm brass nuts and washers.

Variable resistor

VR1 was a 100k miniature preset.

Buzzer

It was found that most of the low cost 6 volt buzzers worked fine but the PCB-mounted type was found to be more secure in the casing.

Switch

SW1 was a SPST toggle switch.

Transistor

The BC108 transistor was used as a simple high-speed electronic switch. As the buzzer tended to be on for short periods there were no real problems with the BC108.

Power supply

It was found that when the circuit was in a waiting state it consumed very little power from the battery.

PCB board

It is important to apply a coat of insulating varnish to the back of the PCB to protect it against moisture which might cause a short circuit.

Components

1 × 100k horizontal miniature preset
1 × 2.2k resistor
1 × 9 V battery connector
1 × BC108 transistor
1 × board (73.6 mm × 55.9 mm)
1 × PCB-mounted buzzer
2 × 120 mm × 3 mm diameter brass rod
2 × 100 mm heat shrink cable
2 × 15 mm diameter plastic beads

CHAPTER SIX   **Mechanisms**

Introduction

Cams are mechanisms that change one type of motion into another. The two types of motion are:

- rotary
- linear.

If a cyclist moves down the road in a straight line this is called linear motion. At the same time the wheels on the bicycle will turn and this is called rotary motion (Figure 6.1).

Figure 6.1 *Rotary and linear motion*

Wheel

A wheel is a round disc that rotates on an axle. The axle is usually an **interference fit** to the wheel. In this case the wheel and axle move as one. If the centre of the wheel is a **clearance fit** then it will rotate on the axle. In this case it is common practice to use a bearing to reduce friction.

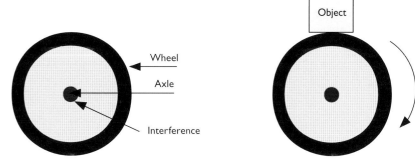

Figure 6.2 *Wheel and Axle*

Figure 6.3 *Rotating wheel*

Cams

If an object is placed on a turning wheel it will rub on its outer edge but will not go up and down. However, if an object is placed on top of a rotating cam it will rise and fall. Cams will also change rotary motion into linear motion.

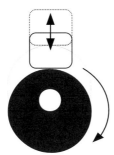

Figure 6.4 *Plate cam*

Most cams are wheel-shaped flat discs with a bump on them or with the axle positioned off-centre. These are called **plate cams** (Figure 6.4). Plate cams have rotary motion but the object resting on the cam moves up and down in reciprocating motion.

Cams are usually made from hardened steel but small plastic and wooden cams can be used if wear is not going to be a problem.

Types of cams

These are the four main types of cam used in technology products:

- circular or eccentric cam
- heart shaped cam
- pear shaped cam
- snail cam.

Circular cams cause the follower to rise and fall at a uniform rate (Figure 6.5).

Heart-shaped cams cause the follower to rise then fall sharply within the area of the groove (Figure 6.6).

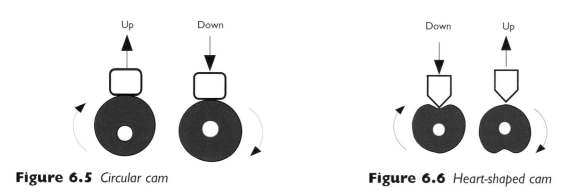

Figure 6.5 *Circular cam*

Figure 6.6 *Heart-shaped cam*

Pear-shaped cams cause the follower to rise suddenly as it comes into contact with the bump part of the cam. This is shown in Figure 6.7. The rise and fall of the object sitting on the cam will happen with equal speed.

Snail cams cause the follower to rise slowly then fall sharply into the step. This is shown in Figure 6.8.

Figure 6.7 *Pear-shaped cam*

Figure 6.8 *Snail cam*

Cam followers

The part that rests on the cam and moves up and down is called the follower (Figure 6.9).

Followers can be made from a range of materials; wood, plastic and mild steel are popular for small products where wear is not a design consideration. When wear must be avoided then the follower would be made from hardened steel.

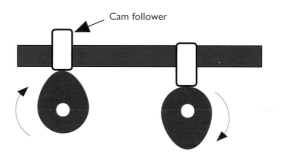

Figure 6.9

There are three main types of followers used with cams:

- flat follower
- knife follower
- roller follower.

Flat followers have a large flat surface at the base of the follower. This surface should be hardened steel to prevent wear. In Figure 6.10 the flat follower is resting on a pear-shaped cam. The follower is in reciprocating motion while the plate cam is in rotary motion.

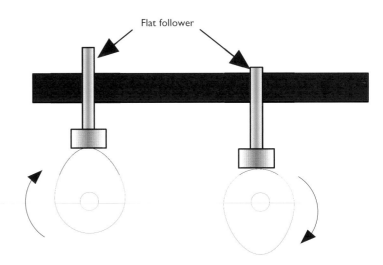

Figure 6.10 *Flat follower resting on a pear-shaped cam*

Roller followers are followers with a small roller bearing at the end. These are used to reduce friction and wear between the follower and the cam. This is shown in Figure 6.11.

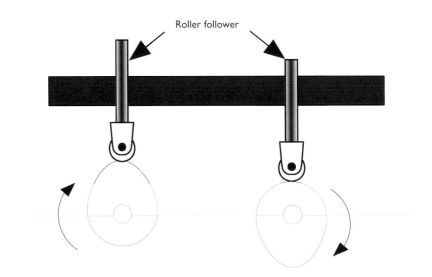

Figure 6.11 *Roller follower sitting on a pear-shaped cam*

Knife followers are mainly used with heart-shaped cams. They have a hardened steel tip and are designed to go into tight curves on the edge of the cams. This is shown in Figure 6.12.

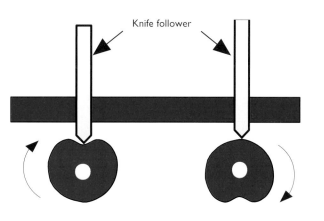

Knife follower

Figure 6.12 *Knife follower resting on a heart-shaped cam*

Example   Cam-operated toy

Design situation

As part of GCSE coursework a student wished to design an educational toy for a younger brother. Early in the investigation it was decided to include movement in the toy to make it more appealing.

Solution

The final solution was the cam-operated dog shown in Figure 6.13.

How it works

As the crank (handle) is turned, the cam on the bottom axle moves round causing the dog's mouth to open and close. Cams are commonly used in this way when movement in one part of the mechanism causes the required movement in another part. Leaving the mechanism open meant the child was able to see how the project worked.

Knowledge of cams and how they work is important in the design and manufacture of this type of product. The following section will explain how the cam and follower were made.

Figure 6.13 *Cam toy*

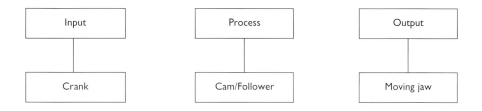

Input	Process	Output
Crank	Cam/Follower	Moving jaw

As the crank is turned the cam rotates, making the follower rise and fall. As the follower rises the mouth closes and as it falls the mouth opens. Figures 6.14 and 6.15 show the operation of the cam.

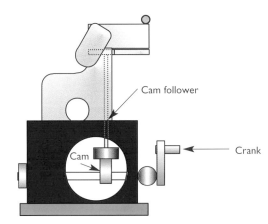

Cam follower

Cam

Crank

Figure 6.14 *Cam in the raised position*

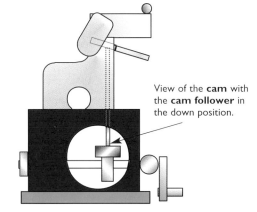

View of the **cam** with the **cam follower** in the down position.

Figure 6.15 *Cam in the down position*

The circular cam was made from a 20 mm beech dowel drilled off-centre. The follower was made from 3 mm and 20 mm beech dowels glued to form a flat follower. Figures 6.16 and 6.17 show the parts of the mechanism.

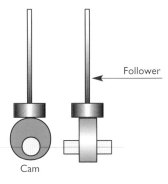

Follower

Cam

Figure 6.16 *Cam and flat follower*

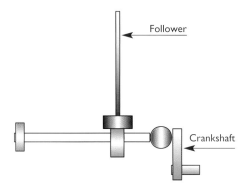

Follower

Crankshaft

Figure 6.17 *Cam–flat follower–crankshaft*

Levers

The lever is possibly the simplest of all the mechanisms to understand. It is used in most machines from the simple builder's crowbar to the handle on a door. One of its functions is to enable a small effort to move a large load.

If you want to lift a heavy box you could place a bar or plank under one edge and push down to make the heavy box rise up. The man in Figure 6.18 is using a bar to lift the box. This bar is called a **lever**. The box is called the **load**.

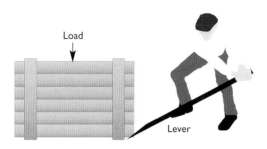

Figure 6.18 *Lifting a heavy object (the load)*

If you try this you will discover that you need to place a small object like a stone or another piece of wood under your lever to make it work. This is called the **fulcrum** for the lever and is shown in Figure 6.19.

When you push down on the lever this is called the **effort** (Figure 6.20). You should also discover that the longer the lever is from the fulcrum, the less effort you will need to lift the box.

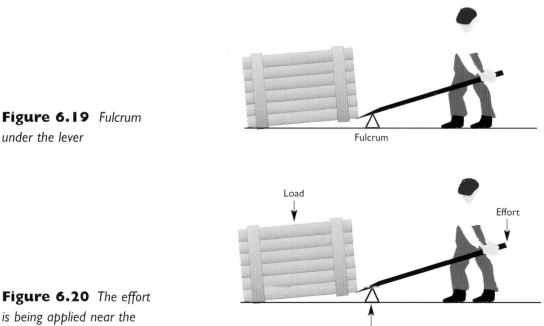

Figure 6.19 *Fulcrum under the lever*

Figure 6.20 *The effort is being applied near the end of the lever*

Classes of lever

There are three main types of levers called classes of lever. These are called class 1, class 2 and class 3 levers.

The type of lever will depend on the positioning of the three parts of the lever: fulcrum, load and effort.

Class 1 lever

This lever has its fulcrum between the load and effort. It is the most common type of lever (Figure 6.21).

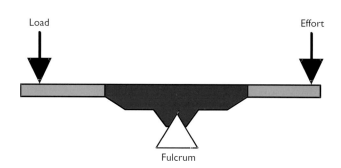

Figure 6.21 *The see-saw is a class 1 lever*

Class 2 lever

Class 2 levers have the fulcrum at one end, the effort at the other and the load in between.

A garden wheelbarrow with rubble in it is a class 2 lever. The axle at the front of the barrow is the fulcrum point, the load is the weight of the wheelbarrow plus its contents, acting downwards, and the effort is made by the person pulling upwards on the handles (Figure 6.22).

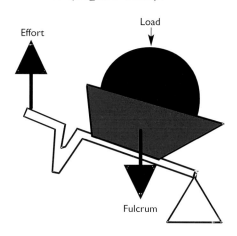

Figure 6.22 *The wheelbarrow is a class 2 lever*

Class 3 lever

This is a lever where the fulcrum is at one end, the load at the other end and the effort in between.

A fishing rod is an example of a class 3 lever. The person fishing holds the rod at one end (fulcrum), the weight of the fish is at the other end (load) and the effort is the pulling on the rod to lift the fish out of the water (Figure 6.23).

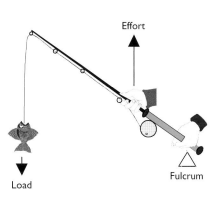

Figure 6.23 *The fishing rod is a class 3 lever*

Drawing levers

Rather than making a drawing of a lever every time, you can draw a symbol to represent it.

The screwdriver being used to open a tin shown in Figure 6.24 is a class 1 lever. If you wanted to draw this as a symbol it would look like Figure 6.25.

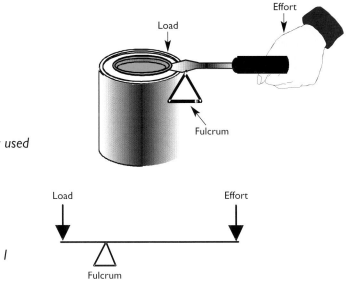

Figure 6.24 *Lever used to remove a lid*

Figure 6.25 *Class 1 lever*

Graphical symbols for class 2 and class 3 levers are shown in Figures 6.26 and 6.27.

A knowledge and understanding of levers can be very useful when designing products. The different classes of levers and the mechanical advantage they can provide will give an insight into levers and what they can do.

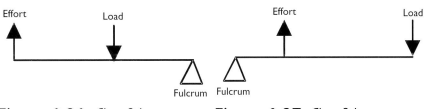

Figure 6.26 *Class 2 lever* **Figure 6.27** *Class 3 lever*

Paint tin lid remover

Design situation

A student's father worked as a painter. Every day the father had the problem of opening tins of paint safely.

Solution

The final solution was a lever that has a hole in one end for fixing it to a keyring. In this way it also acted as a key fob.

Figure 6.28

How it works

The narrow end slides under the lid. The back edge rests on the rim of the tin. When you apply a downward force to the end of the tin opener the tip forces the lid up out of the tin (Figure 6.29).

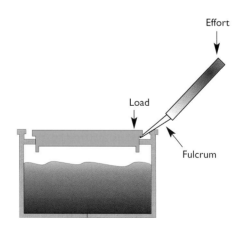

Figure 6.29 *Paint tin opener*

Making the project

Cut a piece of 12 mm wide by 3 mm thick mild steel 100 mm long.

Marking out

Mark a line 30 mm from the end and file the area to form a taper (Figure 6.30).

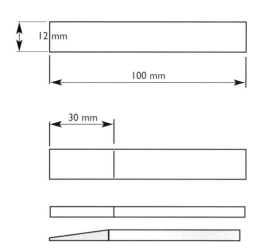

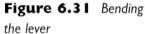

Figure 6.30 *Marking out*

Forming the taper

Hold the work in the vice and file to shape. Then, using a hammer, bend the tapered end to form a 30° slope (Figure 6.31).

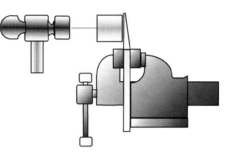

Figure 6.31 *Bending the lever*

Finishing the taper

The taper is now finished with emery cloth.

Finishing

Mask the taper and paint the handle or, better still, if you have access to a plastic fluidisation tank the project can be heated and dipped to form a plastic coated handle.

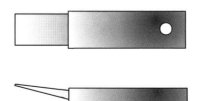

Figure 6.32 *The finished project*

Example

Projects incorporating levers and linkages

It is difficult to think of mechanism projects that do not include linkages and levers.

The following design solutions are the work of two students who were given the brief of 'design an interesting coat-hook that would encourage a younger brother or sister to hang up their coat'. As a starting point they were asked to consider a basic coat-hook (Figure 6.33).

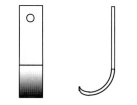

Figure 6.33 *Basic coat-hook*

The two solutions shown are a clown that raises its arms (Figure 6.34) and a dog that raises its ears (Figure 6.35). Both are operated by placing a coat on the hook.

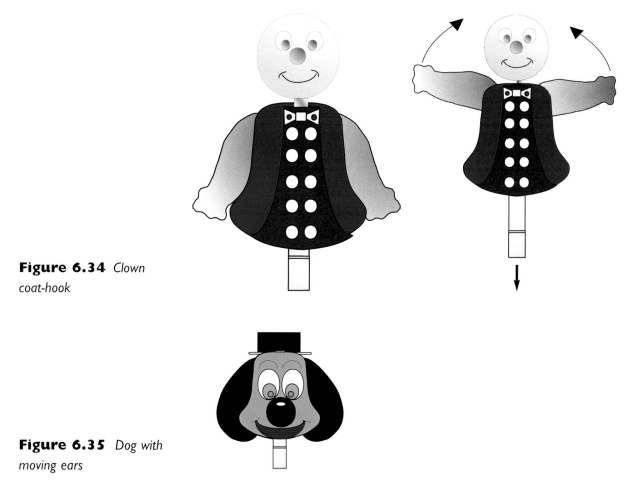

Figure 6.34 *Clown coat-hook*

Figure 6.35 *Dog with moving ears*

Each of the designs incorporate levers and linkages to create movement. The arms and ears are the levers. A piece of string fixed to the ends of the levers acts as a linkage between the levers and the metal coat-hook. When the coat-hook is pulled down, the pivoted arms move down at the top, causing the lower arm to move up with a large movement (Figure 6.36).

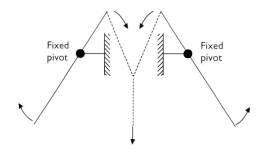

Figure 6.36 *Symbol diagram of the mechanism*

Making the coat-hook

Both designs used the same principle of arms or ears at the side that rise when a coat is placed on the hook.

Body

The design used two 6 mm MDF squares for the body. Two 3 mm holes were drilled for the fixed pivots as shown in Figure 6.37.

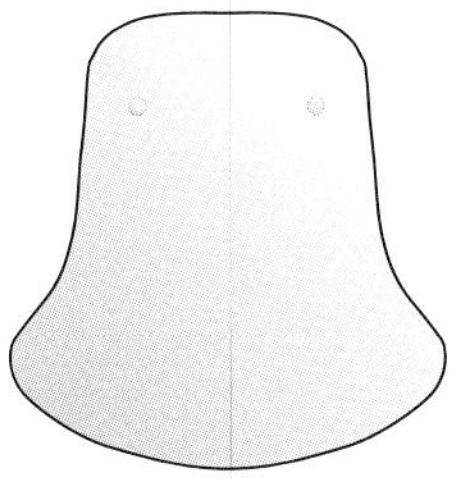

Aluminium hook

The hook was made from 12 mm by 3 mm aluminium that had all the sharp edges filed off.

Guide blocks

The two guide blocks were made from 8 mm square pine cut to a length of 35 mm. The top block was 12 mm long (Figure 6.38).

Figure 6.37 *The body*

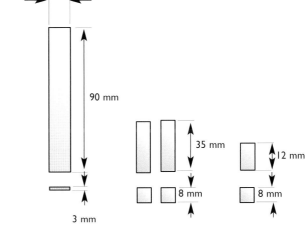

Figure 6.38 *The hook and guide blocks*

Locating the hook

By holding the aluminium bar on the centre line the two guide-blocks were glued in place, making sure that the bar would slide between them (Figure 6.39).

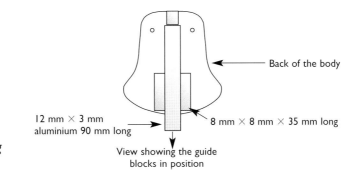

Figure 6.39 *Locating the hook*

Bending the hook

The aluminium hook was bent using the cold bending technique, around a 25 mm metal bar (Figure 6.40).

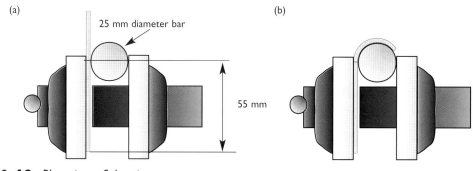

Figure 6.40 *Plan view of the vice*

Loose pivot

A 3 mm hole was drilled in the hook, close to the end of the bar, and countersunk on both sides (Figure 6.41). This was to take the linkages.

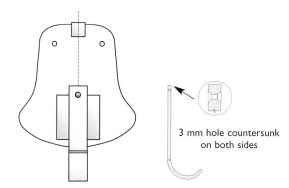

3 mm hole countersunk on both sides

Figure 6.41

Moving parts

Figure 6.42 shows the blanks from which the two moving parts were to be formed. Both had 3.5 mm clearance holes drilled in one end. These were to be the clearance holes for the fixed pivots. Figure 6.43 shows how these blanks are fixed to the backboard.

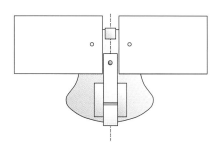

Figure 6.42 *The moving parts are made from these blanks.*

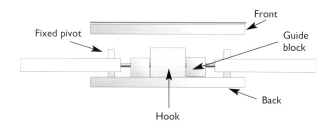

Front

Fixed pivot

Guide block

Back

Hook

Figure 6.43 *View of the top edge of the backboard showing the position of the fixed pivots, hook and guide blocks*

Fixing the linkage

For ease of construction nylon string was used as the linkage.

A hole was drilled in the top of the levers so that a downward pull would cause the ear to rise. The linkage was passed through the hole in the hook before fixing to the levers.

Two 3 mm dowel rods were glued in with the linkages to give a permanent fixing.

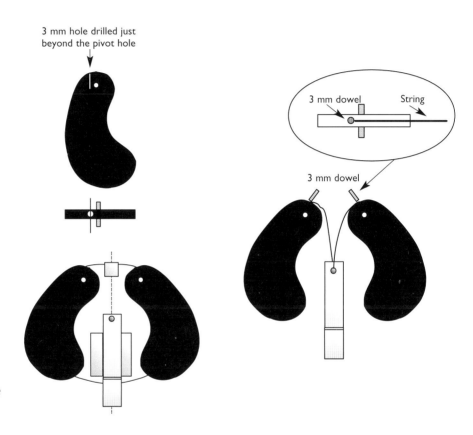

Figure 6.44 *Fixing the string*

The same technique for fixing the string was used with both designs

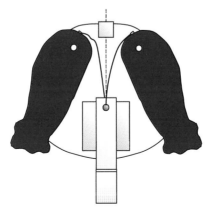

Figure 6.45 *Assembled clown mechanism*

Belts and Pulleys

Belts and pulleys are used in machines. There are several good reasons for using belts and pulleys when designing products containing mechanisms:

- Belts and pulleys transfer motion from one part of the machine to another.
- They can be used to increase or decrease the relative speeds of two shafts.
- Safety: if the load on the drive belt is too great it can slip on the pulley without causing damage to the machine or operator.
- It is easy to change direction between two pulleys using a belt.

The following are some examples of belts and pulleys used in products in the home and school

Pedestal drill

Type of belt: vee

Vee belts are often used on pedestal drills. This can be a major safety feature as the belt can slip on the pulley if the drill bit gets stuck during drilling. If you have the work held firmly in a vice then the slipping action can help prevent you getting injured.

Figure 6.46 *Vee belt used on a pedestal drill*

Washing machine

Type of belt: vee or flat

An electric motor is the drive source for a washing machine. The drive between motor and drum is a belt and pulley. This has the advantage that if the machine is overloaded or clothes get caught between the drums then the belt can slip without damaging the machine.

Figure 6.47 *Flat belt used on a machine*

Vacuum cleaner

Type of belt: round or flat

A vacuum cleaner will use either a round or flat belt to transmit the drive from the motor to the sweeping brushes.
The round belt used on some vacuum cleaners enables the designer to mount the motor at 90° to the brushes. Also, if the brushes catch on the carpet the belt can slip, preventing the carpet and cleaner from being damaged.

Figure 6.48 *Vacuum cleaner drive belt*

Drawing belts and pulleys

Graphical symbol

The graphic symbol for a belt and pulley is shown in Figure 6.49. The centre of the shaft or axle is where the two centre lines in the circles cross.

Pulley direction

The arrows indicate the direction of the belt and the circles indicate the pulleys.

In Figure 6.49 both pulleys are turning clockwise.

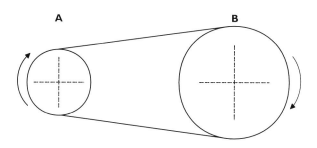

Figure 6.49 *Symbol for a belt and pulley*

In Figure 6.50, pulley A is turning clockwise while pulley B is turning anti-clockwise. Crossover is only possible with a round belt and pulley system.

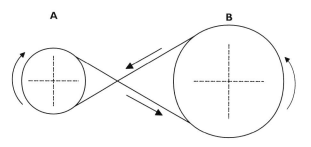

Figure 6.50 *Pulleys turning in opposite directions*

Types of belt

Round belts

Round belts are round in section. They are usually found on light machines where a small drive force is required or when the belt has to turn through 90°.

Vacuum cleaners and CD players often use round belts.

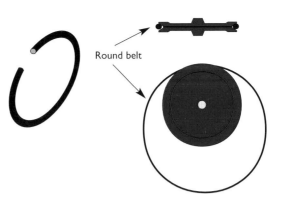

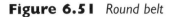

Figure 6.51 *Round belt*

One of the main advantages of the round belt is its ability to twist between shafts that are at 90° or 180° to each other (Figure 6.52).

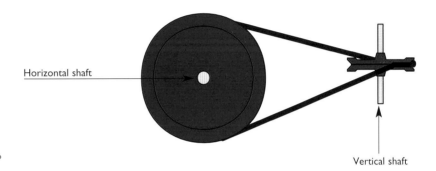

Figure 6.52 *Shafts at 90°*

Vee belts

With the vee belt you have a larger area of the belt in contact with the pulley. This increases the friction between the two and enables you to have a greater drive force before the belt starts to slip (Figure 6.53).

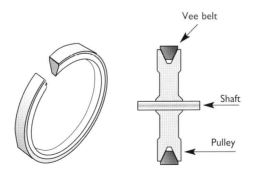

Figure 6.53 *Vee belts*

Shaft speed

If pulleys of different diameters are placed on two shafts then the shafts can be made to turn at different speeds. The pulley that provides the power is called the **driver pulley**, while the one on the output shaft is the **driven pulley**. In Figure 6.54 the driver pulley is smaller than the driven pulley. In this case the driver pulley at the motor (10 mm diameter) will have to turn four revolutions before the driven pulley (40 mm diameter) completes one revolution.

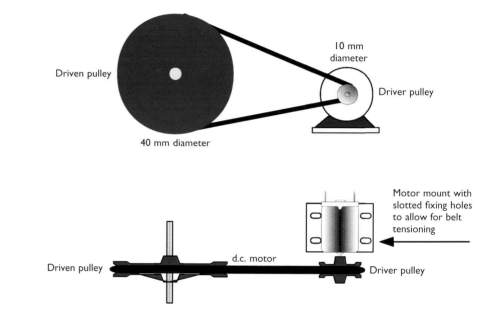

Figure 6.54 *Shaft speed*

Stepped cone pulleys

If pulleys of different diameters are placed on the same shaft then the shaft can be made to turn at different speeds. In the example shown in Figure 6.55 a four-stepped cone pulley system is used. An electric motor is the power source. The pulleys on the shaft of the electric motor will be the driver pulleys.

A stepped cone pulley can be found on pedestal drills. It is used to change the speed of the output shaft. By moving the vee belt downward on the pulleys you will make the output shaft run more slowly.

When the vee belt is on the top pulleys the output shaft is at its maximum speed (Figure 6.55).

When the vee belt is on the bottom two pulleys the output shaft is at its slowest speed (Figure 6.56).

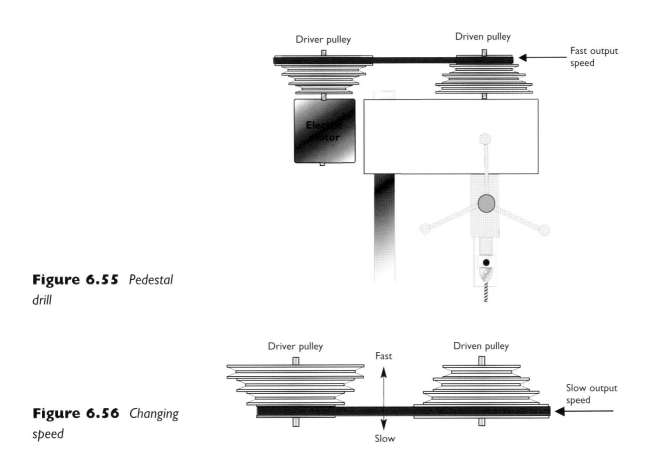

Figure 6.55 *Pedestal drill*

Figure 6.56 *Changing speed*

Tensioning belts using motor mounts

When a belt is passed around a pulley you must make sure it is tight. This is called applying tension. The simplest method of doing this is to mount the motor so that it can slide to increase the tension.

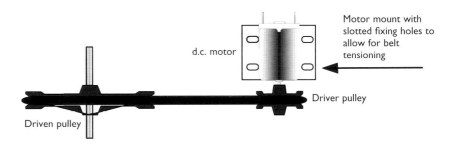

Figure 6.57 *Motor mounts*

Gears

Gears are designed to transmit motion from one shaft to another. Unlike belts and pulleys, which enable the belt to slip on the pulley, gears provide precise non-slip motion between shafts.

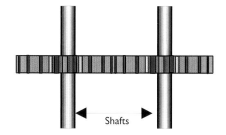

Figure 6.58 *Gears transmit motion between shafts*

Gears are wheels that have teeth on the outer edge. These teeth are designed to fit together. When two or more gears fit correctly we call this **meshing** (Figure 6.59).

Figure 6.59 *Meshed gears*

When two or more gears mesh this is called a **gear train**. Two or more gears meshed side by side is called a simple gear train (Figure 6.60).

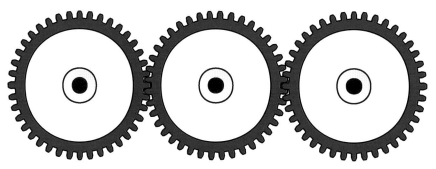

Figure 6.60 *Simple gear train using three gears*

Spur gears

Gears like those shown in Figure 6.61 which connect parallel shafts are called **spur gears**. The smaller wheel is called the **pinion**. The larger is called the **gear wheel**.

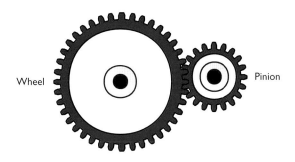

Wheel

Pinion

Figure 6.61 *Spur gears*

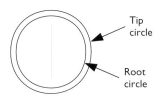

Tip circle

Root circle

Figure 6.62 *Graphic symbol for a gear wheel*

Drawing gears

The graphic symbol for a gear is two circles with a centre cross where the centre of the shaft would be. The outer circle represents the tip of the tooth. The inner circle represents the bottom or root of the tooth (Figure 6.62).

When two or more gears mesh then the symbols overlap so that the tip circle of one gear touches the root circle of the adjoining gear. The graphic symbol is shown in Figure 6.63.

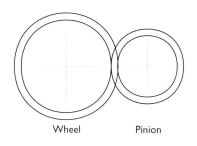

Wheel   Pinion

Figure 6.63 *Meshed spur gears*

As well as showing the front view of the gears it is sometimes necessary to show gears on their edge. The graphic symbol for meshed gears on their edge forming a simple gear train is shown in Figure 6.64.

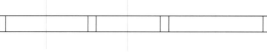

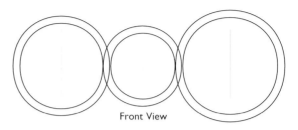

Plan View

Front View

Figure 6.64 *Symbol for three meshed gears viewed from the front and from the top (plan view)*

Direction of gears

When you have two gears meshed together, one gear will go clockwise while the other goes anti-clockwise. In the example shown in Figure 6.65, the driver gear is turning anti-clockwise. This makes the driven gear turn clockwise.

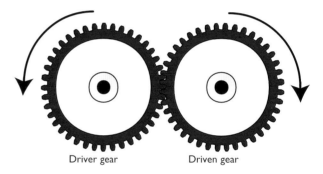

Driver gear   Driven gear

Figure 6.65 *Direction of rotation*

If you have three gears in the train then the first and last gear will turn in the same direction. In Figure 6.66 the yellow and red gears are turning in the same direction. The centre gear is called an **idler gear**.

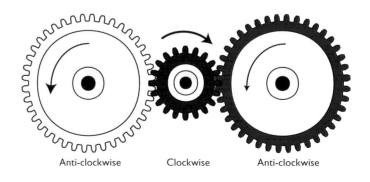

Anti-clockwise   Clockwise   Anti-clockwise

Figure 6.66 *Changing direction using an idler gear*

Calculating the gear ratio

Sometimes you will need to know how fast the driven gear is turning in relation to the driver gear. This is called calculating the gear ratio.

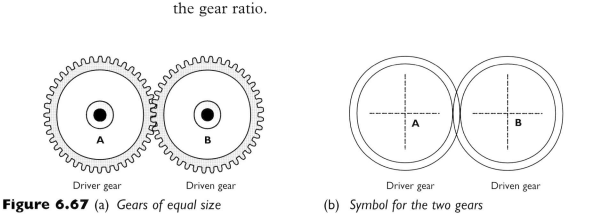

Figure 6.67 (a) *Gears of equal size*   (b) *Symbol for the two gears*

If you consider the two gears in Figure 6.67, gear A has 40 teeth and gear B has 40 teeth. If gear A turns through one revolution gear B will also turn through one revolution. To calculate the gear ratio we use the formula:

$$\text{Gear ratio} = \frac{\text{number of teeth in the driven gear}}{\text{number of teeth in the driver gear}} = \frac{40}{40} = \frac{1}{1}$$

Gear ratio = 1:1

If you change the size of the driver gear to 20 teeth, as shown in Figure 6.68, then you will change the speed of the driven gear. This can be calculated using the same formula.

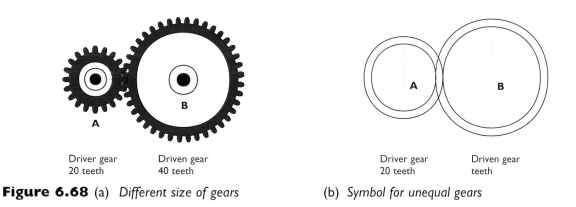

Figure 6.68 (a) *Different size of gears*   (b) *Symbol for unequal gears*

$$\text{Gear ratio} = \frac{\text{number of teeth in the driven gear}}{\text{number of teeth in the driver gear}} = \frac{40}{20} = \frac{2}{1}$$

Gear ratio = 2:1

The driver gear will now turn twice for every single turn of the larger driven gear.

Calculating the gear ratio of a simple gear train

When calculating the gear ratio of a simple gear train incorporating three gears you would use the same formula as for two gears.

$$\text{Gear ratio} \quad = \frac{\text{number of teeth in the driven gear}}{\text{number of teeth in the driver gear}}$$

However, this time you will have to consider the gears in pairs of driven divided by driver, with A as the first driver gear.

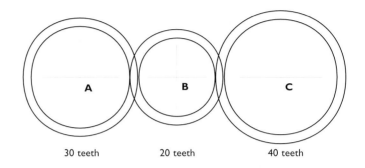

Figure 6.69 *Calculating the gear ratio for a simple gear train*

30 teeth   20 teeth   40 teeth

$$\text{Gear ratio} \quad = \frac{\begin{array}{c}\text{number of teeth in}\\ \text{the driven gear B}\end{array}}{\begin{array}{c}\text{number of teeth in}\\ \text{the driver gear A}\end{array}} \times \frac{\begin{array}{c}\text{number of teeth in}\\ \text{the driven gear C}\end{array}}{\begin{array}{c}\text{number of teeth in}\\ \text{the driver gear B}\end{array}}$$

$$= \frac{B}{A} \times \frac{C}{B}$$

$$= \frac{20}{30} \times \frac{40}{20} = \frac{800}{600} = \frac{8}{6} = \frac{4}{3}$$

Gear ratio $\quad = \quad 4{:}3$

Notice that this is the same as the gear ratio for A and C if B were not there.

Idler gear

In a simple gear train the middle gear is called an idler gear. The idler gear does not change the speed of the final driven gear. The function of the idler gear in Figure 6.70 is to enable the rotational direction of the driven gear to change. In the example shown, the idler gear enables the driven gear to turn in the same direction as the driver gear.

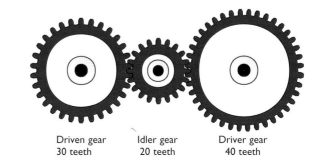

   Figure 6.70 *Idler gear*

Driven gear   Idler gear   Driver gear
30 teeth   20 teeth   40 teeth

Introduction

Computer control allows you to use the computer to control external devices. Devices such as electric motors, lamps, buzzers, relays, buggies, robotic arms, LEDs and many others can be connected to the computer. A robotic arm, which uses computer control designed by a student is shown in the photograph.

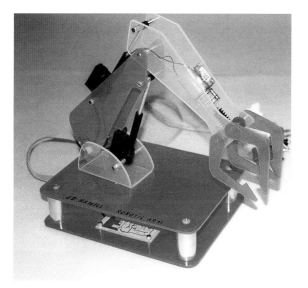

Control software

This is a program that you can use with your computer to control external devices. There are a number of specially written software packages on the market and these can be purchased through educational supply companies. Alternatively, you could write your own programs and many students still do this using basic or machine code programming language. However, the time you would need to learn the language is considerable.

Control interfacing

Under no circumstances should you directly connect external devices to your computer. To do so may, and most likely will, result in you damaging the computer beyond repair. You must always connect your project through an **interface**.

An interface is a device designed to protect your computer. Most will also amplify (increase) the electrical signal coming from the computer. It will also enable you to make physical connections to the computer easily and safely.

Figure 7.1 shows a typical commercial interface. It has eight input sockets, eight output sockets, four motor sockets and a switch that allows you to amplify the signal from the computer to either 6 or 12 volts.

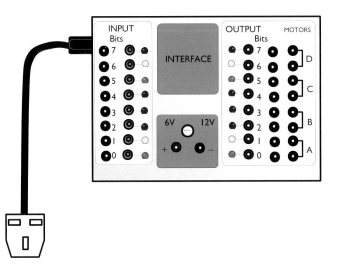

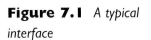

Figure 7.1 *A typical interface*

With this or similar interfaces you can connect up to eight sensors to the inputs and up to eight output devices. D.C. motors can be connected to the motor sockets. This will enable you to make the motors turn both clockwise and anti-clockwise. If you plan to use the motor sockets you should be aware that the corresponding output sockets will then not be available.

Input–process–output

All but the most basic control systems will have input–process–output and computer control is no different. Consider a computer system in terms of input–process–output:

Input: Press a key, this is an input via the keyboard.

Process: After the key is pressed the input is processed in the CPU (central processing unit).

Output: The signal from the keyboard is processed and the letter is displayed on the screen. Therefore the output device is the monitor.

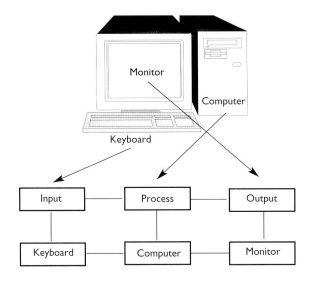

Figure 7.2 *Computer input–process–output*

Microprocessor systems

Microprocessors/computers have a number of building blocks that are linked to each other. These are the CPU, ROM, RAM, I/O and A-D. The interconnection between these building blocks is shown in Figure 7.3.

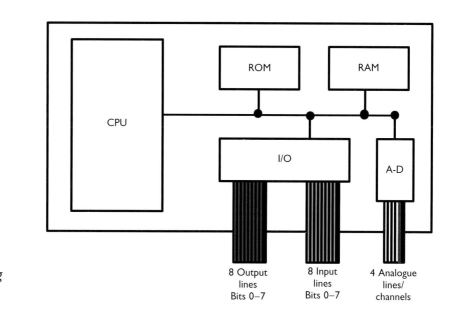

Figure 7.3 *Micro-processor/computer building blocks*

8 Output lines Bits 0–7

8 Input lines Bits 0–7

4 Analogue lines/ channels

CPU (Central Processing Unit)

It is the job of the CPU to handle and process all the information coming into the computer and then do something with it. The CPU can only do its job if it has other supporting ICs (integrated circuits). It is the job of these other ICs to store and handle vital information.

ROM (Read Only Memory)

The function of the ICs containing ROM is to hold vital information necessary for the running of the microprocessor/computer. The term 'read only memory' means that the CPU can only read this information but cannot add to or remove information from it.

RAM (Random Access Memory)

When you put information into a microprocessor/computer it is held in the RAM. You can add to and remove information from the RAM. For example, as you type a letter the words are held in the RAM. The CPU can then access this information if and when it is needed, for example to send a completed letter to the printer.

Here input–process–output usually refers to the system being controlled by the computer. If you consider the set of traffic lights shown in Figure 7.4 the input will be the push switch that starts the sequence. The output will be the lights. The process will happen in two places:

- the CPU
- the interface.

The CPU processes the signal and runs the program. The interface takes the small signal from the computer and amplifies it to turn on the traffic lights.

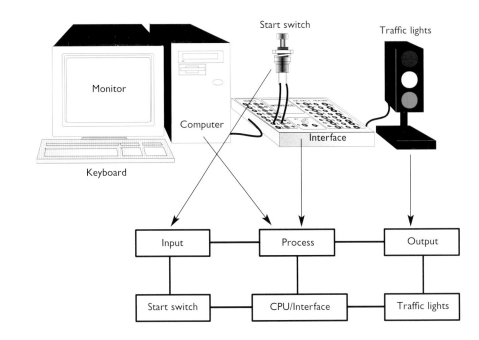

Figure 7.4 *Input–process–output for traffic lights*

Outputs

Most microprocessors/computers can have eight output lines (wires) connected to them (Figure 7.5). These lines can be programmed to come on and off as required using the appropriate software. Each line is called a **bit** and they are numbered 0 to 7. The voltage at each line is 5 volts but the current will be very small so this needs to be increased (amplified) to a meaningful level if you wish to turn on output devices such as lamps, motors and buzzers.

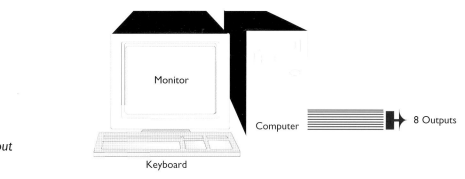

Figure 7.5 _8 × output lines, bits 0–7_

Amplifying the output signal

To amplify a signal means to increase either the current or voltage or both. This can be achieved by using a transistor as shown in Figure 7.6.

The output line is bit 0. This comes from the computer at 5 volts. It is used to turn on a transistor that is connected to a 12 volt secondary power supply. It is important to connect both zero volts together.

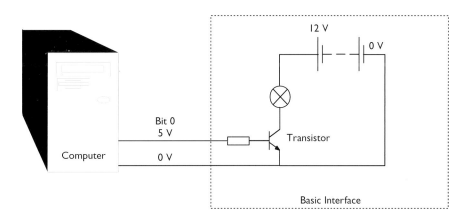

Figure 7.6 _Amplifying an output signal_

Connecting Output Bits 0–7

So far only one output bit is connected to the interface. To connect all eight you would simply repeat the circuit shown in Figure 7.6. The circuit would then be housed in a box for protection. This box is called an interface.

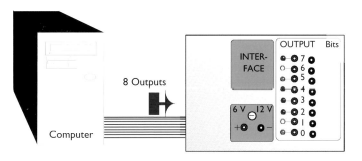

Figure 7.7 _Housing the outputs_

It is possible for your computer to detect an input signal and respond in some way. Most computers will allow you to connect eight inputs called bits. Each bit is identified by a number from 0 to 7.

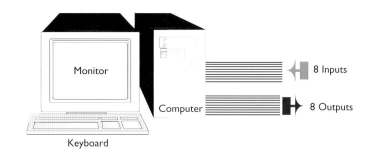

Figure 7.8 *8 × input lines, bits 0–7*

Detecting an input signal

The term input would seem to imply that you have to send a signal (voltage) into the computer. This is not strictly true; what you are actually doing is making the computer detect the closing or opening of a switch. The power for the switch comes out of the computer and all you have to do is connect a switch between this line and zero volts. This is shown in Figure 7.9.

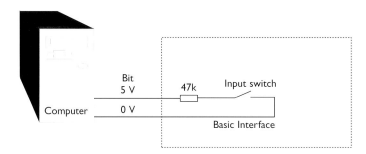

Figure 7.9 *Detecting an input signal*

A high signal of 5 volts comes out of the computer. A switch is connected between the 5 volts and 0 volts. When the switch is closed the computer will detect the fall in voltage and identify this as a low signal. The 47k resistor is used to prevent a short circuit between 5 volts and 0 volts when the switch is closed.

Connecting input bits 0–7

Figure 7.9 shows one input line bit 0 connected to a basic interface. This would be repeated for all eight input lines, bits 0–7. The circuit would then be housed in a protective box similar to the one shown in Figure 7.10.

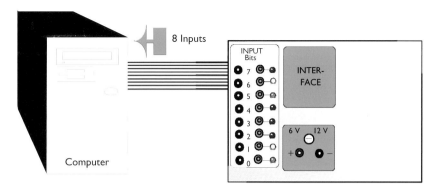

Figure 7.10 *Housing the inputs*

Digital Input/Output Interface

The interfaces explained so far have been **digital interfaces**. This means that they can detect an input that is on or off (high or low). They can also turn an output on or off. By combining both the output and input interfaces in one housing you have a digital input/output interface. On commercial interfaces 4 mm sockets are commonly used to enable you to plug in your input switches and output devices. Some commercial interfaces also have status LEDs to indicate when an input/output is high or low.

A typical commercial digital input/output interface is shown in Figure 7.11. This interface has additional output motor sockets for driving a small d.c. motor forward and reverse.

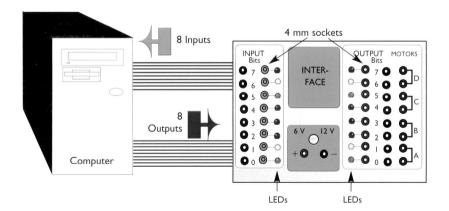

Figure 7.11 *8 × input/output digital interface*

Flowcharts for digital input/output

You can use a flowchart to help you plan the sequence of your microprocessor/computer control program. There are a number of common symbols used in flowcharts to represent conditions such as start, stop, output, decisions, wait and loops. These symbols are shown on the next page.

Start/Stop/End

Use the Start symbol at the beginning of your program/sub-routine or procedure. Use the Stop symbol to stop your program. Use the End symbol to end a sub-routine or procedure

Output

Use the Output symbol to turn on or off outputs.

Decision

Use the decision symbol for all inputs. Digital input signals, analogue signals, comparing the value of variables in a loop, are all inputs. Decision symbols usually have a yes/no arrow out from them and denote whether or not the decision has happened or not.

Process

Use the process symbol for time delays and variables.

Sub-routine

Use the Sub-routine symbol for calling a sub-routine into your main program. Some software packages call this Macros or Procedures.

An example of the use of flowchart symbols is shown in Figure 7.12.

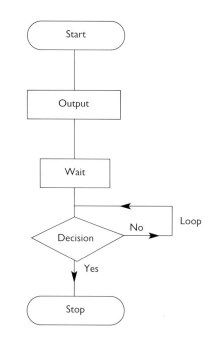

Figure 7.12 *Flowchart symbols*

Output summary

In addition to using the correct symbols in your flowchart it is necessary to give a summary of what you want to happen at each stage of the program.

If you wished to write a program to turn on bit 0 you would have to give the output cell a name and specify the condition of each bit. This is shown in Figure 7.13. The summary is then shortened to O/P 0 0 0 0 0 0 0 1.

Figure 7.13 *Output summary*

Decision summary

Decisions are mainly associated with inputs. If you wished to include a decision in your program that waited until input bit 0 was high, then you would give the decision cell a name and specify the condition of the input bit. The program would check to see if this condition was true and if it was, the program would do something; if not it would keep checking until it was true. An example is shown in Figure 7.14. Once again the summary would be shortened to read I/P 0 0 0 0 0 0 0 1.

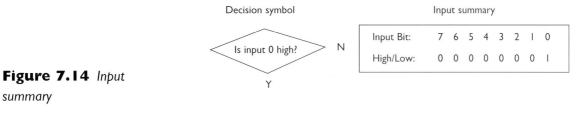

Figure 7.14 *Input summary*

Wait summary

If you want to have a time delay in your program flowchart you would use the wait symbol. It is usual to specify the wait in seconds or parts of a second. An example of the summary for this is shown in Figure 7.15.

Figure 7.15 *Wait summary*

Programming Model Race Car Start lights

Design situation

A student was asked to design a set of start lights for use with model racing cars. The lights had to come on when the input switch was pressed. The light sequence was to be red, red/amber then green.

Figure 7.16 *Racing track*

Solution

A set of model traffic lights was made which included a push-to-make switch and three coloured bulbs. Each of the three lights was connected to the output bits 0–2 on the interface. Green was connected to bit 0, amber was connected to bit 1 and red was connected to bit 2. The switch was connected to input bit 0. A photo of the lights is shown in Figure 7.17.

Figure 7.17 *Lights for model car racing*

Flowchart

The flowchart in Figure 7.18 shows the basic sequence for the lights.

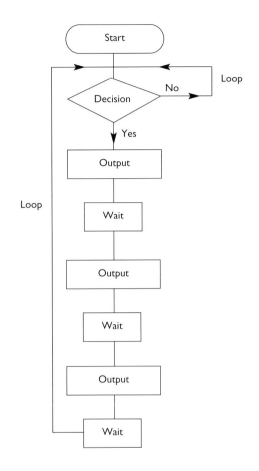

Figure 7.18 *Symbols used in the flowchart*

The flowchart in Figure 7.19 shows the final sequence. This was set out so that the program would start, then go round in a loop until the input switch was pressed. Once this input was true then the program moved down to turn on the first output red light. A wait of 1 second was then added so that the light would stay red for one second. Next the red and amber came on together for 2.5 seconds before the green go light came on. The green light remained on for 10 seconds after which time the program looped back to the start to wait for another input.

Figure 7.19 shows what is happening at each stage of the program.

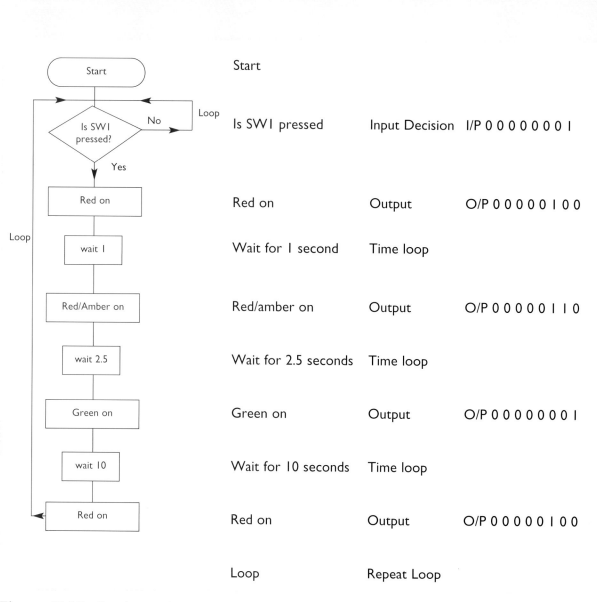

Figure 7.19 *Flowchart and programming details*

Christmas tree

Design situation

Christmas decorations can become uninteresting if they just sit there doing nothing. There is a need for a Christmas decoration that will be controlled by a computer. This will enable it to be programmed so that the lights come on and off in different patterns.

Solution

The solution was an electronic Christmas tree with eight lights.

The lights were LEDs and each one was connected to an output port on the computer interface. The final solution can be seen in Figure 7.20.

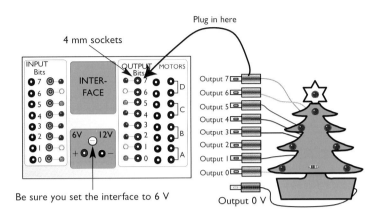

Figure 7.20 *Computer controlled christmas tree*

Making the Christmas tree

The tree was made on a PCB. Each LED was soldered to the board with the negative leg to the outside so that there was a common negative (Figure 7.21).

Figure 7.21 *Connecting the LED*

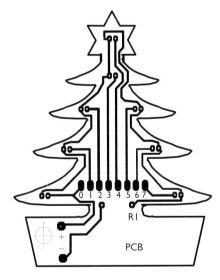

Figure 7.22 *Back of the PCB*

Connecting to the computer

The positive leg of each LED was soldered to the inside tracks. Each LED had a wire connected to it and a 4 mm plug joined to the end. These were then plugged into the interface.

The current limiting resistor R1 is 74R and the voltage should be 5–6 volts.

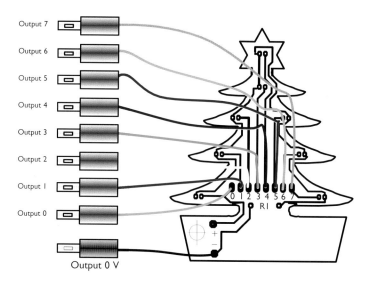

Figure 7.23 *PCB connected to output lines*

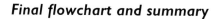

Final flowchart and summary

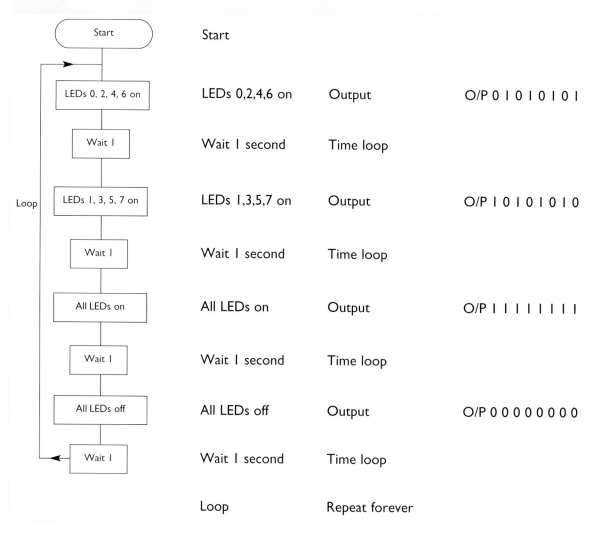

Start	Start		
LEDs 0, 2, 4, 6 on	LEDs 0,2,4,6 on	Output	O/P 0 1 0 1 0 1 0 1
Wait 1	Wait 1 second	Time loop	
LEDs 1, 3, 5, 7 on	LEDs 1,3,5,7 on	Output	O/P 1 0 1 0 1 0 1 0
Wait 1	Wait 1 second	Time loop	
All LEDs on	All LEDs on	Output	O/P 1 1 1 1 1 1 1 1
Wait 1	Wait 1 second	Time loop	
All LEDs off	All LEDs off	Output	O/P 0 0 0 0 0 0 0 0
Wait 1	Wait 1 second	Time loop	
Loop	Loop	Repeat forever	

Figure 7.24 *Flow chart and programming details*

Cycle shop display

Design situation

A local cycle shop owner wanted a counter top display that would come on 5 seconds after a customer walked into the shop. The display had to run for just under 1 minute.

Figure 7.25 *Cycle shop*

Solution

The solution was a computer controlled model cyclist. A push-to-make switch fixed to the shop door activated the display. After 5 seconds the display started to turn. A reed switch was fixed to the cycle's rear frame and the magnet inserted in the wheel. This provided a second input that was used to count the revolutions of the rear wheel. Three separate lines were used in the flowchart (Figure 7.27) to determine when the count was equal to or greater than 100. These were: setting A as a variable, increasing the value of A by one each time the program moved past a certain point and by setting up a decision that checked the value of the variable A.

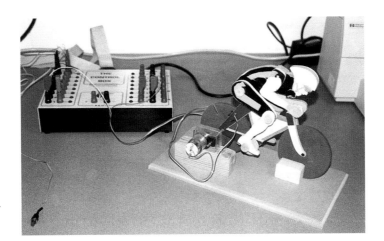

Figure 7.26 *Picture of the cycle shop display*

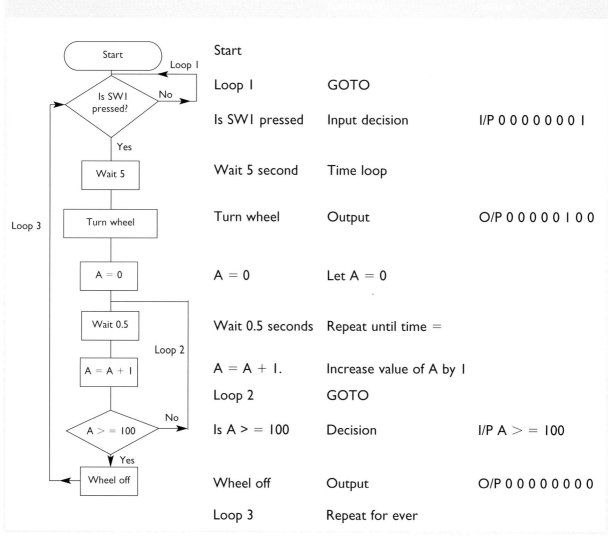

The following table shows the flowchart elements and their corresponding programming details:

Flowchart	Operation		Input/Output
Start	Start		
Loop 1	Loop 1	GOTO	
Is SW1 pressed?	Is SW1 pressed	Input decision	I/P 0 0 0 0 0 0 0 1
Wait 5	Wait 5 second	Time loop	
Turn wheel	Turn wheel	Output	O/P 0 0 0 0 0 1 0 0
A = 0	A = 0	Let A = 0	
Wait 0.5	Wait 0.5 seconds	Repeat until time =	
A = A + 1	A = A + 1.	Increase value of A by 1	
	Loop 2	GOTO	
A >= 100	Is A >= 100	Decision	I/P A >= 100
Wheel off	Wheel off	Output	O/P 0 0 0 0 0 0 0 0
	Loop 3	Repeat for ever	

Figure 7.27 *Flowchart and programming details*

CHAPTER EIGHT　**Pneumatics**

Introduction

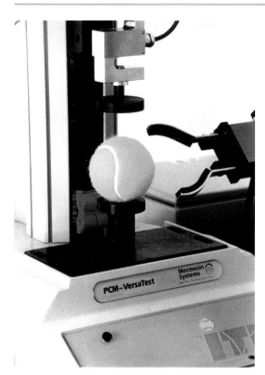

Figure 8.1 *Rig for testing tennis balls*

Pneumatics is a system that operates with compressed air. A simple pneumatic device is the compressed air drill used by dentists for drilling teeth. Industry uses pneumatics in the manufacture of a range of components. The car industry uses robots with pneumatic cylinders that open and close to lift and place components onto cars as they are being assembled. Some tennis ball manufacturers use pneumatics to lift and place balls into a test rig.

The main advantage of pneumatics is that it will repeat the operation accurately over and over again. The main disadvantage can be the noise and the need for special compressors.

Safety

When working with pneumatic equipment it is important to work safely. Compressed air is a form of stored energy and when released incorrectly it can do serious damage to you and others. So always exercise caution when using it.

The following are a few simple safety rules you should follow.

Compressor system

Do ensure that this is in good working order before you use it. A qualified engineer should check the complete system at least once a year.

Figure 8.2 *Compressed air system*

Do not use equipment if you are in any doubt about its condition.

Do ensure the pressure at the compressor is set correctly. Just enough pressure to operate the system should be used, 6–7 bar is adequate for most school use.

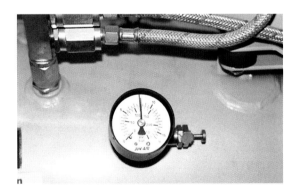

Figure 8.3 *The reservoir pressure gauge*

Figure 8.4 *The line pressure gauge*

Do ensure the pressure in the line is set correctly, 4–5 bar is adequate for school workshops.

Workstation

Do ensure the pressure at your workstation is set correctly. Set it as low as is practical to operate your system. For small-bore components used in school for modelling purposes 2–3 bar should be adequate. You can set this by adjusting the air pressure regulator at your station.

Do not connect the main air supply to your system until you have checked all components and pipes are connected correctly. Only the operator should turn on the system.

Do not continue to operate the system if you notice air leaking from any joint or component.

Do turn off the main air supply to your system before making alterations.

Moving parts

Do keep your fingers away from all moving parts.

Do not blow compressed air at anyone as this can result in serious injury.

Do ensure all pipes are connected, as loose pipes will thrash around when the air supply is turned on.

Figure 8.5 *Manifold, pressure gauge and regulator*

The Pneumatic 3/2 valve

One of the basic components of any pneumatic circuit is the pneumatic valve. Valves act like electrical switches in that they are designed to turn something on. Valves can be used to perform the simple task of switching on or off the main air supply.

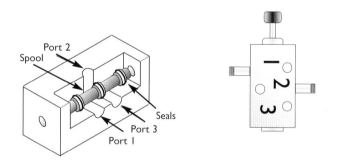

Figure 8.6 *A 3/2 pneumatic valve*

There are two main types of valves you will use in pneumatics. These are 3/2 valves and 5/2 valves. The 3/2 valve gets its name because it has three ports (holes) and is capable of changing between two states. State one is when it **actuated**, that is, the air at port 1 passes through the valve and out through port 2. The second state is **un-actuated**; this is when the air is exhausting through port 2 and port 3.

Air flow through 3/2 valves

The spool in Figure 8.7 is moved by air. These valves are called **pilot/pilot air operated 3/2 valves**. The air moving the spool is called **signal air**.

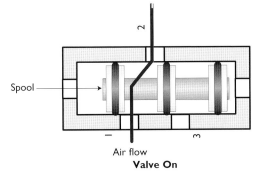

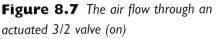

Valve On

Figure 8.7 *The air flow through an actuated 3/2 valve (on)*

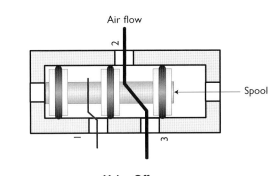

Valve Off

Figure 8.8 *The air flow through an un-actuated 3/2 valve (off)*

Drawing 3/2 valves

A 3/2 valve has three ports. Each port has a specific function. Port 1 is where the main air comes in. Port 2 is the output port when the valve is actuated (turned on). Port 3 is the exhaust.

Figure 8.9 shows the symbol for a 3/2 valve in the actuated (on) state. In this state the air comes in port 1 and goes out port 2. Also shown is a sectional drawing through a 3/2 valve in this state.

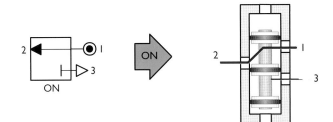

Figure 8.9

Figure 8.10 shows the symbol for a 3/2 valve in the off state. A sectional drawing of the valve is also shown. In this state the valve allows air to pass through port 2 and out port 3.

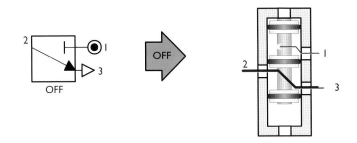

Figure 8.10

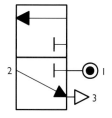

Figure 8.11 *Symbol for a 3/2 valve*

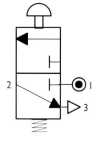

Figure 8.12 *Push-button/spring return 3/2 valve*

Symbol for a 3/2 valve

When you draw the symbol for a 3/2 valve you must show both the on and off states. It is usual to show the actuated (on) position of the valve at the top and the un-actuated (off) position at the bottom. The symbol for a 3/2 valve is shown in Figure 8.11.

Operating valves

No diagram of a valve is complete without showing the means of operation. The 3/2 valves and 5/2 valves used in pneumatics can be operated using a number of different mechanical or electrical operators.

Symbol for a push-button/spring return 3/2 valve

Pushing the button on top of the valve operates this valve (Figure 8.12). When the button is released the spring inside the valve makes it return to the off position.

It is common to see this valve labelled as a push-button operated 3/2 valve.

Symbols for mechanically operated 3/2 and 5/2 valves

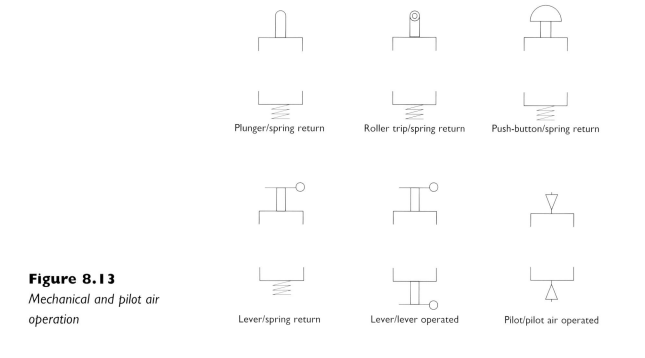

Figure 8.13

Mechanical and pilot air operation

Plunger/spring return   Roller trip/spring return   Push-button/spring return

Lever/spring return   Lever/lever operated   Pilot/pilot air operated

Single-acting cylinders

A single-acting cylinder is a pneumatic output device that requires compressed air to make the piston move out. When the air is removed a spring causes the piston to return. The out stroke is called the positive stroke and the return stroke is called the negative stroke.

Figure 8.14 shows a single-acting cylinder with part of the cylinder cut away to let you see inside.

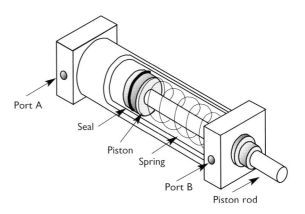

Figure 8.14 *Cut-away drawing of a single-acting cylinder*

How it works

Air coming in port A will cause the piston to move out. Remove the air pressure and the spring will push the piston back again.

The seal around the piston prevents the air from escaping over the piston. Port B allows the air in front of the piston to escape. This is called the **exhaust**.

Symbol for single-acting cylinder

When you want to draw a single-acting cylinder it is not necessary to draw what it looks like. Instead you draw the symbol for it. This is shown in Figure 8.15.

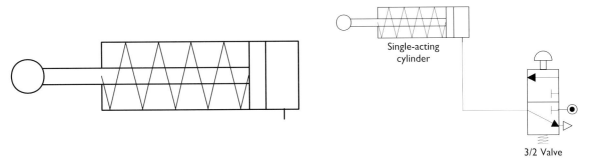

Figure 8.15 *Symbol for a single-acting cylinder*   **Figure 8.16** *Circuit diagram for a single-acting cylinder*

The circuit diagram for a single-acting cylinder being controlled by a 3/2 valve is shown in Figure 8.16.

When the piston and piston rod is moving out we call this **going positive**. When the piston and piston rod is going in we call this **going negative**.

Cylinder off

When no air is present at the back of the piston the spring keeps it in the negative position (Figure 8.17).

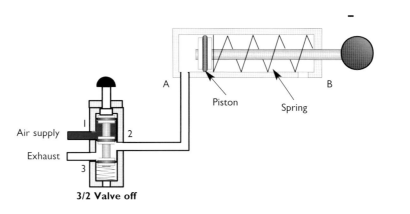

Figure 8.17 *Cylinder negative*

Cylinder going positive

Press the 3/2 valve and compressed air arrives at the back of the piston (port A). This makes the piston move out with a certain force.

The air in the cylinder in front of the piston is allowed to escape through a small vent hole at the front of the cylinder (port B) (Figure 8.18).

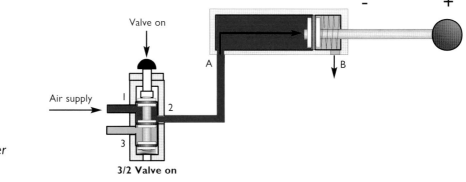

Figure 8.18 *Cylinder positive*

Cylinder going negative

When the 3/2 valve is released the spring inside the cylinder forces the piston back to a negative position. The escaping air is called the exhaust and passes through the 3/2 valve via port 2 to port 3 (Figure 8.19).

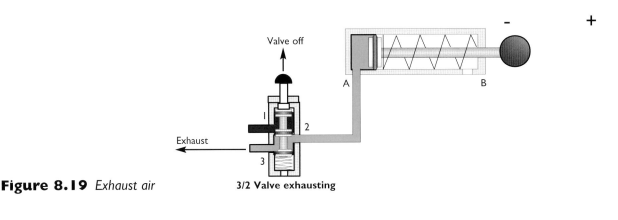

Figure 8.19 *Exhaust air*

| Example | **Single-acting cylinder used to open and close a bus door** |

Design situation

A bus company which operates a fleet of school buses would like to change its manually operated doors to pneumatically operated ones. This will allow the driver to remain in his/her seat when opening the door.

Figure 8.20 *School bus*

Solution

The final design used a single-acting cylinder actuated by a push button spring return 3/2 valve. A model of the bus was made to show how the system would operate.

Figure 8.21 *The model bus*

The door was pulled open by means of a single-acting cylinder as shown in Figure 8.22.

The spring in the single-acting cylinder caused the door to close automatically when the air was removed from the cylinder (Figure 8.23).

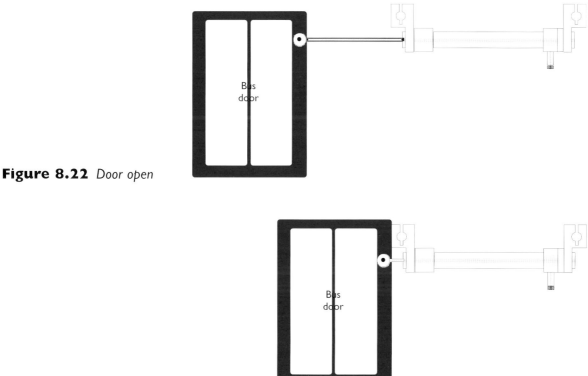

Figure 8.22 *Door open*

Figure 8.23 *Door closed*

Circuit diagram for the bus door

A circuit diagram for the bus door is shown in Figure 8.24. When the push button/spring return 3/2 valve is actuated (on) the main air at port 1 passes through the valve and out port 2. This causes the single-acting cylinder to go positive.

When the button is released the spring inside the cylinder causes it to go negative closing the door.

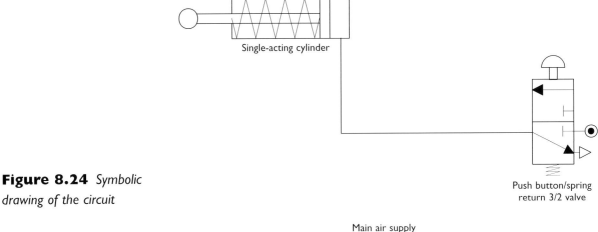

Figure 8.24 *Symbolic drawing of the circuit*

Single-acting cylinder

Push button/spring return 3/2 valve

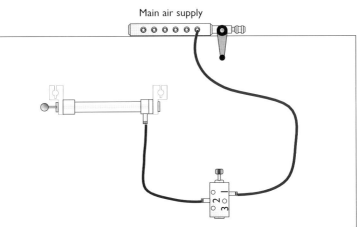

Main air supply

Figure 8.25 *Real world view of the circuit before it was fitted to the model bus*

Valves in 'OR' logic

Example **Modifying the bus door circuit**

It was decided to modify the circuit for the bus door to include a push button on the outside of the bus, so that pupils entering the bus could also open the door.

SELB SCHOOL

Figure 8.26

Figure 8.27 shows the modified circuit. When either valve **A** or valve **B** is pressed the cylinder will go positive. When valves are arranged in this way they are said to be in an **OR logic** combination. When this is added to the original circuit design the driver inside the bus or the pupils outside the bus can open the door.

Complete Technology and Design

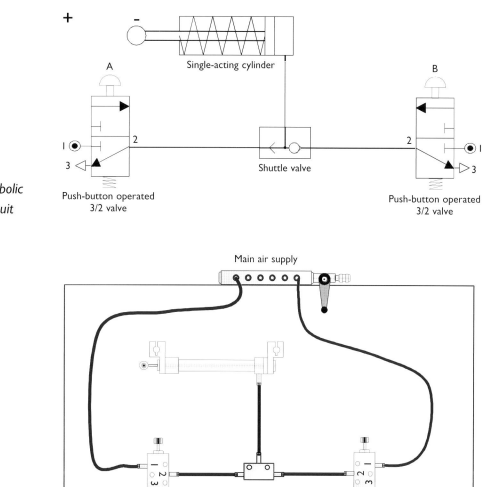

Figure 8.27 *Symbolic drawing of an OR circuit*

Figure 8.28 *View of the modified circuit*

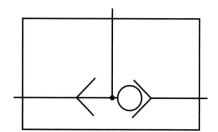

3/2 Valve A   Shuttle valve   3/2 Valve B

Shuttle valves

The shuttle valve is the component that is at the heart of circuits that include the **OR logic** functions. A shuttle valve is shown in Figure 8.29 and its symbol in Figure 8.30.

Figure 8.29 *Shuttle valve*   **Figure 8.30** *Symbol for a shuttle valve*

How the shuttle valve works

Inside the shuttle valve there is a small rubber spool that moves from side to side. In Figure 8.31 the spool in the shuttle valve is forced over to the left by the air flowing through valve B. When this happens air is able to flow through the shuttle valve to the cylinder.

When valve A is pressed first, the spool will move to the right allowing the air to pass through and flow into the cylinder (Figure 8.32).

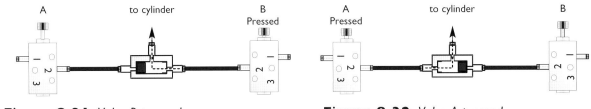

Figure 8.31 *Valve B pressed*   **Figure 8.32** *Valve A pressed*

Speed control using a one-way flow restrictor valve

It is good practice where possible to restrict the cylinder's exhaust.

Example	**Improving the bus door design**

When the bus door was operated it was found to open very quickly. It was decided to use a one-way flow restrictor to control the speed of the air going into the single-acting cylinder (going positive). The modified circuit diagram can be seen in Figure 8.33.

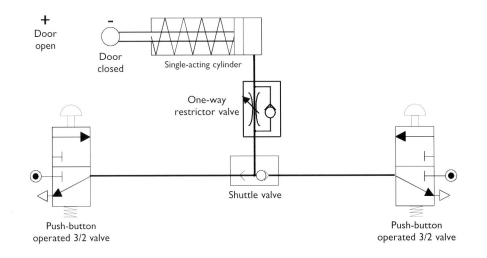

Figure 8.33 *Circuit diagram of the OR logic circuit with a one-way restrictor valve added*

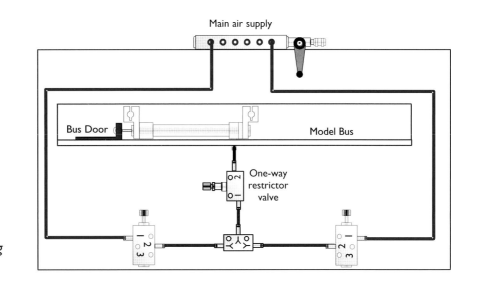

Figure 8.34 *Modelling the bus door*

Flow restrictor valves

There are two main types of restrictor valve: one-way and two-way (bi-directional).

One-way flow restrictor

A one-way restrictor valve is shown in Figure 8.35 and its symbol is shown in Figure 8.36. The arrow at the ball shows the direction in which the air is restricted by the valve.

Figure 8.35 *A one-way restrictor valve*

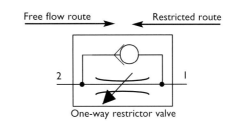

Figure 8.36 *Symbol for a one-way restrictor valve*

How it works

The one-way restrictor valve will allow the air to flow freely through it in the direction port 2 to port 1. This happens because the ball is pushed back, compressing the spring. This enables the air to flow freely in the direction of the arrow (Figure 8.37).

When the air is flowing in the direction of port 1 to port 2 then it must pass through the narrow chamber at the tip of the screw. The size of the opening can be increased or decreased by turning the adjuster screw. The air coming in port 1 forces the ball against the seals to prevent the air going down this free flow route (Figure 8.38).

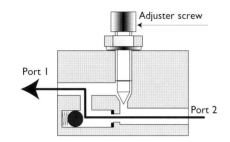

Figure 8.37 *Sectional view showing the free flow route*

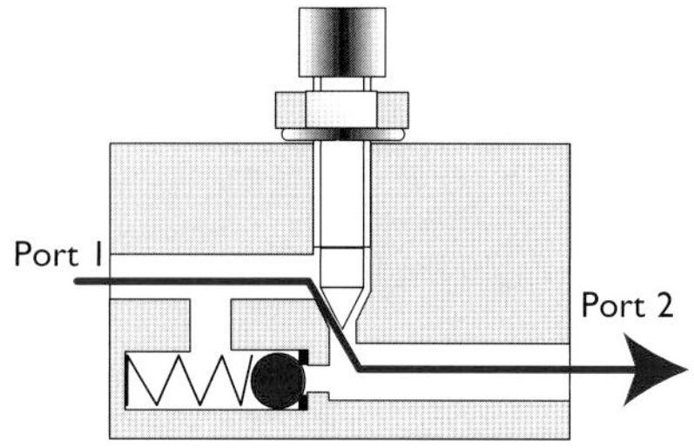

Figure 8.38 *Sectional view showing the restricted route*

Two-way restrictor

A two-way restrictor valve will control the speed of the cylinder going positive and negative by restricting the flow of air passing down the pipe. The restriction is equal in both directions. The symbol for a two-way restrictor is shown in Figure 8.39.

How it works

The air passing through the restrictor valve has to flow past a cone shaped chamber. The adjuster screw can be raised or lowered to open or close this chamber. A small opening will restrict the flow of air in both directions (Figure 8.40).

Figure 8.39 *Symbol for a two-way flow restrictor*

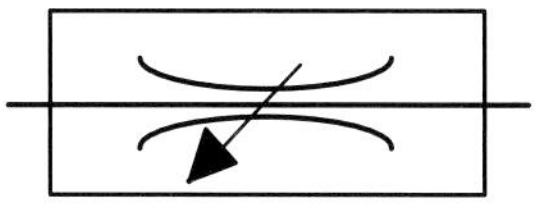

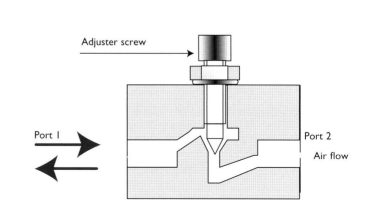

Figure 8.40 *Sectional view of a two-way restrictor*

Valves in 'AND' logic

You can arrange two valves in series to create an AND logic function. Figure 8.41 shows a circuit designed to operate with AND logic function. Only when both valves are pressed will the single-acting cylinder go positive.

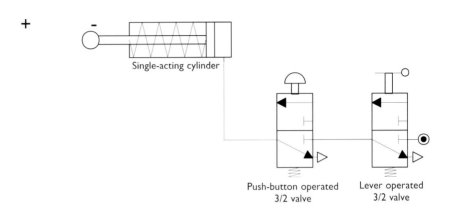

Figure 8.41

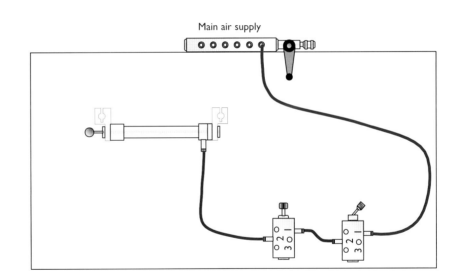

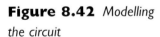

Figure 8.42 *Modelling the circuit*

The main use for the AND arrangement of two valves is in situations where safety is important.

In Figure 8.43, AND logic is used to ensure the guillotine's safety guard is down before the machine comes on. The single-acting cylinder will only come down to cut the paper (positive stroke) when the guard is down and the manual button is pressed.

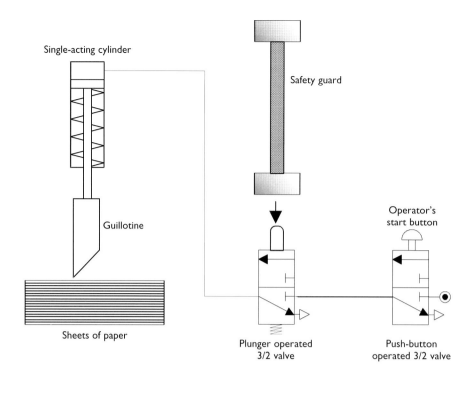

Figure 8.43

| Example | **Bus door circuit** |

The AND logic function could be added to the bus door circuit as a safety feature for the driver (Figure 8.44). It could be part of the handbrake system so that the bus must stop and the handbrake be put on before the driver can open the door.

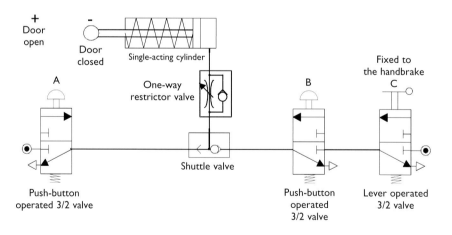

Figure 8.44 *AND/OR logic circuit for bus door*

How it works

When the bus has come to a stop the driver pulls on the handbrake, which actuates valve C. The driver can now press valve B to open the door. Valves C *and* B must be actuated to open the door from inside the bus.

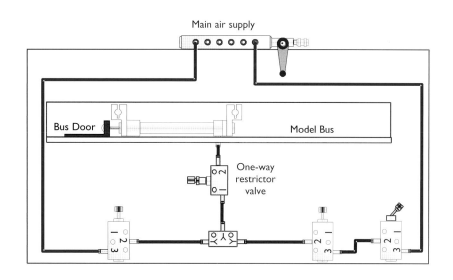

Bus Door

Model Bus

One-way
restrictor
valve

Figure 8.45 *View of the model bus with AND/OR logic and cylinder speed control*

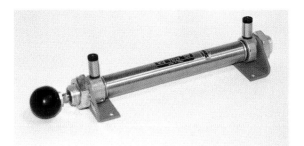

Figure 8.46 *View of the model bus*

Double-acting cylinders

Figures 8.47 and 8.49 show a double-acting cylinder. The symbol for a double-acting cylinder is shown in Figure 8.48. This type of cylinder requires air pressure at port A to make it go positive. If the air pressure is removed the cylinder will remain in a positive position. To make the cylinder go negative again air pressure must be present at port B. The air is prevented from going over the piston by the seal.

Figure 8.47 *Double-acting cylinder*   **Figure 8.48** *Symbol for a double-acting cylinder*

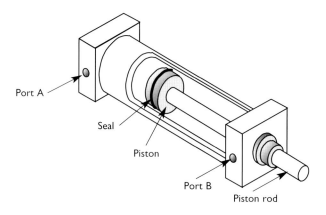

Figure 8.49 *Cut-away view of a double-acting cylinder*

Two 3/2 valves could be used to control the double-acting cylinders (Figure 8.50). When valve A is pressed the cylinder will go positive. This valve must be released before valve B is pressed. Pressing valve B will cause the cylinder to go negative. Air present in the cylinder can exhaust through valve A.

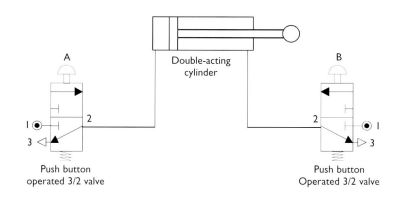

Figure 8.50 *Circuit diagram for a double-acting cylinder*

The Pneumatic 5/2 valve

It is not normal to control a double-acting cylinder using two 3/2 valves as shown in Figure 8.50. This is usually done with a 5/2 valve. The 5/2 valve would replace the two 3/2 valves. A lever operated 5/2 valve is shown in Figure 8.51.

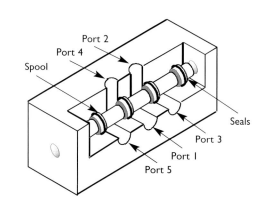

Figure 8.51 *A lever operated 5/2 valve*

Figure 8.52 *Cut away view of a 5/2 valve*

Drawing 5/2 valves

As with other pneumatic components it is not necessary to draw the actual valve when designing a circuit. You would draw the symbol (Figure 8.56). A 5/2 valve means five ports and two states. The states are air in port 1 and out port 2 or, in port 1 and out port 4.

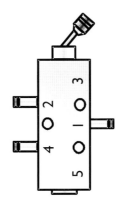

Figure 8.53 *Drawing of a lever operated 5/2 valve*

5/2 valve with ports 1 and 4 open

The symbol for this state is shown in Figure 8.54.

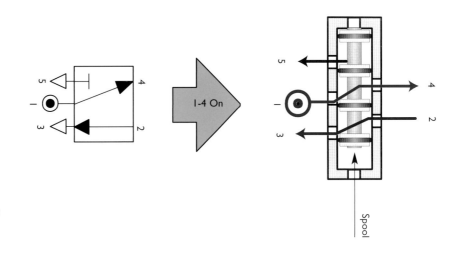

Figure 8.54 *Ports 1–4 open*

5/2 valve with ports 1 and 2 open

The symbol for this state is shown in Figure 8.55.

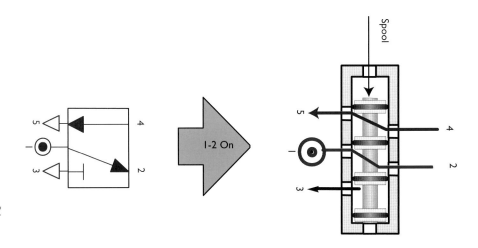

Figure 8.55 *Ports 1–2 open*

Symbol for a 5/2 valve

The graphic symbol for a 5/2 valve must include both sets of port combinations (Figure 8.56). This symbol does not show the means by which the spool inside the valve is made to move.

The symbols for mechanical and electrical switching are the same for both 3/2 valves and 5/2 valves (see Figure 8.13).

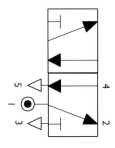

Figure 8.56 *Symbol for a 5/2 valve*

Double-acting cylinder controlled by a lever/spring return 5/2 valve

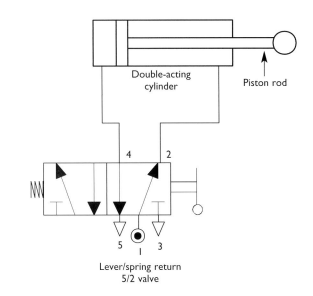

Figure 8.57 *Circuit diagram for a lever/spring return 5/2 valve*

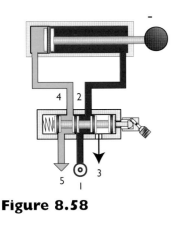

Figure 8.58

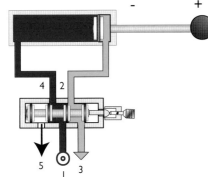

Figure 8.59

Figure 8.60 'T' piece

How the valve works

Cylinder going negative

When the spool is in the position shown in Figure 8.58 then the main air will come in port 1 and out at port 2. When this happens the compressed air forces the piston back into the negative position. The exhaust passes out through ports 4 and 5.

Cylinder going positive

When the spool is in the down position then the main air will come in at port 1 and out at port 4 (Figure 8.59). When this happens the compressed air forces the piston out into the positive position. The exhaust passes out through ports 2 and 3.

Controlling two double-acting cylinders from one 5/2 valve

This circuit will require two 'T' pieces to connect both cylinders in parallel. A 'T' piece is shown in Figure 8.60. When two air lines are joined in this way the diagram should show a small black dot to indicate the connection. Crossover lines are drawn one on top of the other without the dot. A circuit diagram in which two double-acting cylinders are controlled by a 5/2 valve is shown in Figure 8.61.

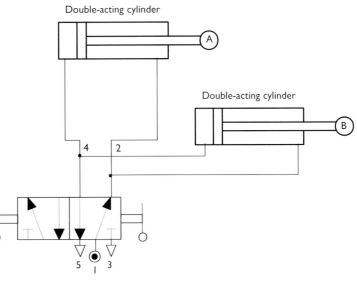

Figure 8.61 *Controlling two cylinders*

Lever/lever operated 5/2 valve

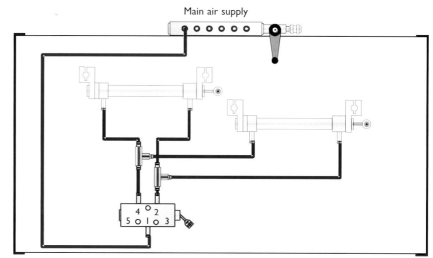

Main air supply

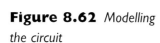

Figure 8.62 *Modelling the circuit*

Real world view of the completed circuit

Pilot/pilot air operated 5/2 valves

So far we have used a lever operated 5/2 valve to control the double-acting cylinder. This next circuit uses a pilot/pilot air operated 5/2 valve to control the double-acting cylinder. This is the commonest method for controlling a double-acting cylinder. A pilot/pilot air operated 5/2 valve is shown in Figure 8.63. The spool inside the 5/2 valve is moved by air pressure rather than by mechanical means. This air pressure is called signal air and is represented by a dotted line on the diagram.

Figure 8.64 shows a pilot/pilot air operated 5/2 valve changed by means of two push-button operated 3/2 valves.

Figure 8.63 *A pilot/pilot air operated 5/2 valve*

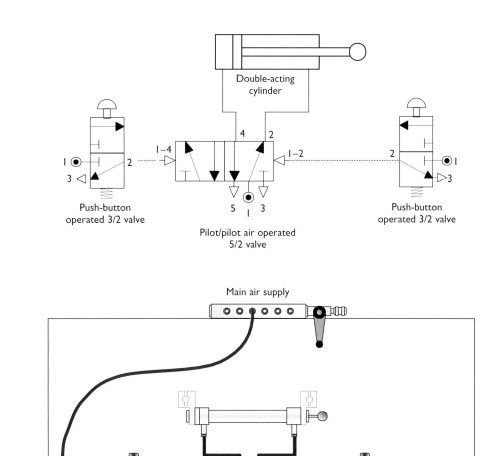

Figure 8.64

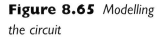

Figure 8.65 *Modelling the circuit*

Automatic return

You can use the air signal from a 3/2 valve to *automatically* change the state of the pilot/pilot air operated 5/2 valve.

In the example shown in Figure 8.66 the push-button operated 3/2 valve starts the cycle. This makes the double-acting cylinder go positive. A plunger operated 3/2 valve is pressed by the piston rod at the end of the positive stroke. When this happens, air passes through the 3/2 valve down to the end of the 5/2 valve, causing the spool inside to change state. The valve changes from a 1–4 to a 1–2 combination.

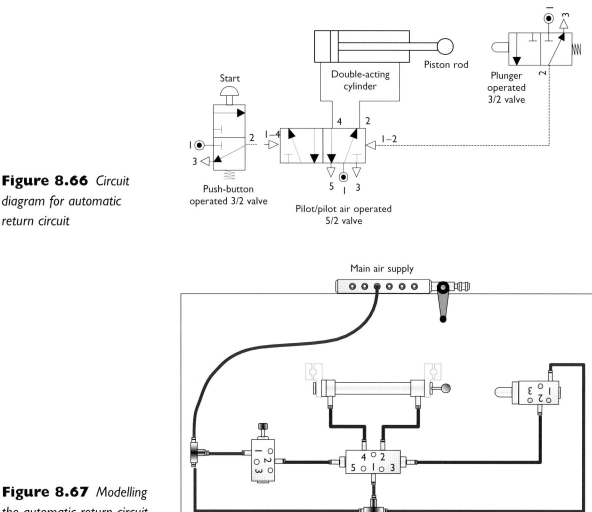

Figure 8.66 *Circuit diagram for automatic return circuit*

Figure 8.67 *Modelling the automatic return circuit*

Time Delay circuit

There will be times when it is necessary to have a small time delay in your circuit. The circuit in Figure 8.68 has a time delay between the time when the piston rod hits the plunger operated 3/2 valve and the cylinder going negative.

The time delay is achieved by using a reservoir and one-way restrictor valve. A reservoir is simply an empty container. The one-way restrictor valve controls the rate of fill. By decreasing the amount of air passing through the restrictor valve you can increase the time it takes to fill the reservoir. Only when the reservoir is full will the air be able to flow down the second half of the pipe with enough force to change the pilot/pilot air operated 5/2 valve.

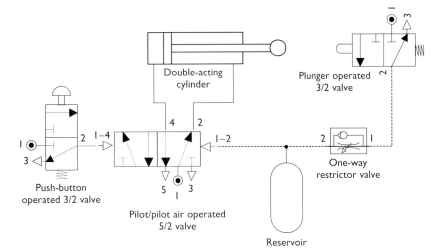

Figure 8.68 *Time delay circuit*

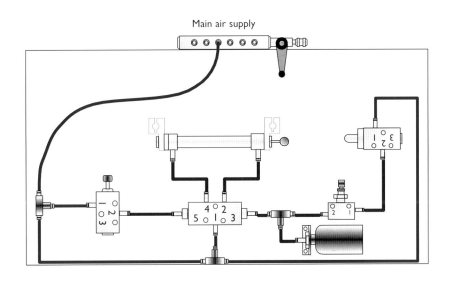

Figure 8.69 *Modelling a time delay circuit*

| Example | **Conveyor system** |

Figure 8.70 *A reservoir*

Design situation

A manufacturer of portable and wide screen television sets would like to sort these by size into two different containers. The boxes come down the same conveyor and are currently hand-sorted down their respective conveyors into the containers.

You are asked to design an automatic system to sort the boxes.

Solution

The solution was to have a roller trip 3/2 valve set at the edge of the conveyor. Only the large boxes would activate this valve. When the valve was pressed, a time delay would ensure enough time for the box to reach conveyor 2 before the cylinder pushed the divider to change the direction of the outgoing boxes.

Once the boxes reached a second 3/2 valve the box would cause the valve to activate the 5/2 valve to give a 1–2 state again. The circuit for the conveyer system is shown in Figure 8.71.

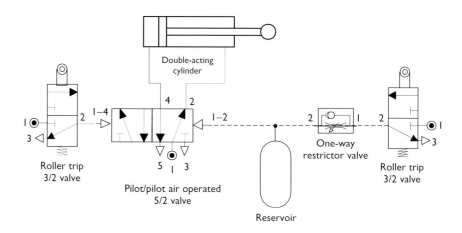

Figure 8.71 *Circuit diagram for the conveyor system*

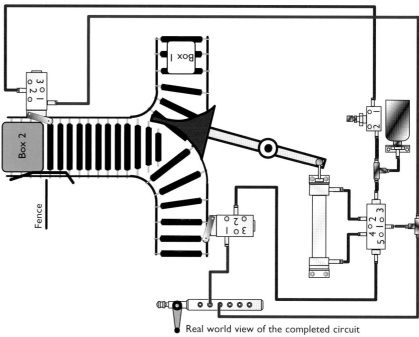

Figure 8.72 *Modelling the conveyor system*

Diaphragm Operated 3/2 Valves

Diaphragm operated 3/2 valves are similar to mechanical valves such as the push-button operated valve. With the push-button valve you have to press the spool inside the valve down with your hand. The diaphragm operated 3/2 valve has a small soft plastic membrane inside a chamber. Figure 8.73 shows a diaphragm operated 3/2 valve. Its symbol is shown in Figure 8.74.

Figure 8.73 *Diaphragm operated 3/2 valve*

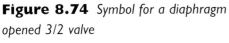

Figure 8.74 *Symbol for a diaphragm opened 3/2 valve*

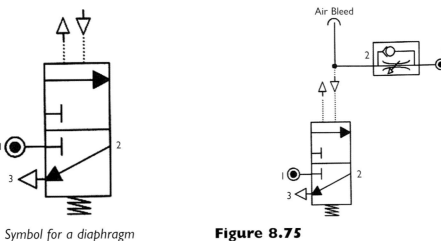

Figure 8.75

When the diaphragm is inflated it pushes down the spool in the same way as the push-button did. To make the diaphragm inflate you have to use a one-way restrictor and a T piece.

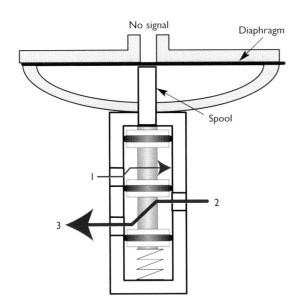

Figure 8.76 *Diaphragm when no signal is present*

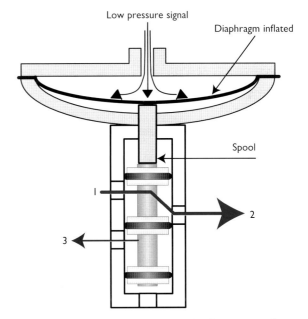

Figure 8.77 *Diaphragm inflated when a signal is present*

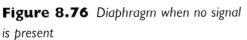

The restrictor allows just enough air to go down to the diaphragm and at the same time allows some to escape out into the atmosphere. The pipe used for the escaping air is called an **air bleed**. To make the valve actuate (come on) you must block this air bleed. This will send all the air down to the diaphragm, inflating it.

Diaphragm start/automatic return

Cover the air bleed pipe and the air is forced down to turn on the diaphragm 3/2 valve. An air signal flows along to the pilot/pilot air operated 5/2 and creates a 1–4 airflow through it. Air flowing out of port 4 causes the double-acting cylinder to go positive (Figure 8.78). At the end of the positive stroke the piston rod hits the plunger operated 3/2 valve. Air passes through this valve and flows along to create a 1–2 air flow through the 5/2 valve. Air flowing out of port 2 causes the double-acting cylinder to go negative.

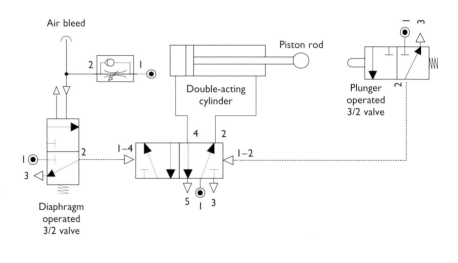

Figure 8.78 *Circuit diagram of a diaphragm 3/2 valve used to make the piston go positive*

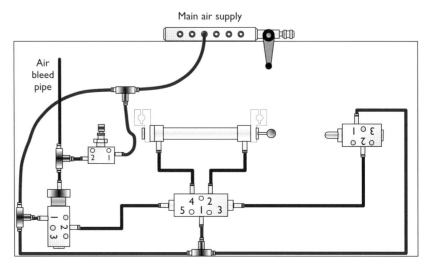

Figure 8.79 *Modelling the circuit*

Single-acting cylinder controlled by a diaphragm operated 3/2 valve

In this circuit (Figure 8.80) the diaphragm operated 3/2 valve is used in conjunction with a one-way restrictor valve and an air bleed, to control a single-acting cylinder.

The main advantage of this type of circuit is that the 3/2 valve will actuate with physical contact: all you need to do is block the escaping air.

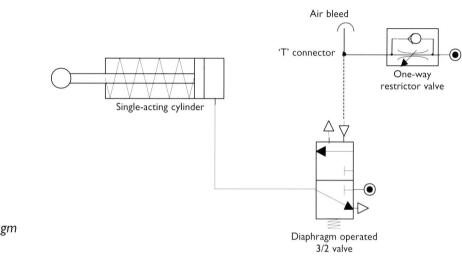

Figure 8.80 *Circuit diagram using a diaphragm operated 3/2 valve*

Example Conveyor belt system

The system in Figure 8.81 is designed to push the boxes from conveyor belt 1 on to conveyor belt 2 using two single-acting cylinders. The cylinders will go positive when the box blocks the air bleed at the end of belt 1.

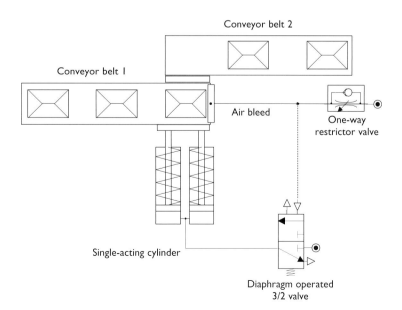

Figure 8.81 *Conveyor system*

Reciprocating Motion

Reciprocating motion happens when the piston goes positive and negative automatically.

It is possible to create reciprocating motion using two roller trip 3/2 valves, a double-acting cylinder and a pilot/pilot air operated 5/2 valve. This is shown in Figure 8.82. The 3/2 valves alternately provide the air signals that change the state of the 5/2 valve from 1–2 to 1–4 port combinations repeatedly, until the air is switched off. Main air passing through the 5/2 valve causes the double-acting cylinder to go positive and negative.

Care is needed when testing this circuit as it immediately becomes active as soon as the main air supply is turned on.

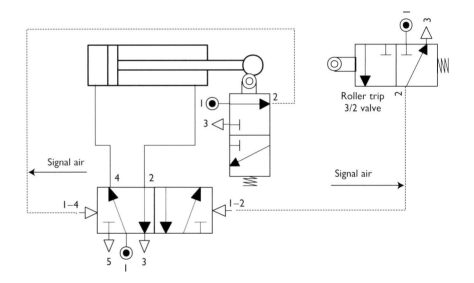

Figure 8.82 *Circuit diagram for reciprocating motion*

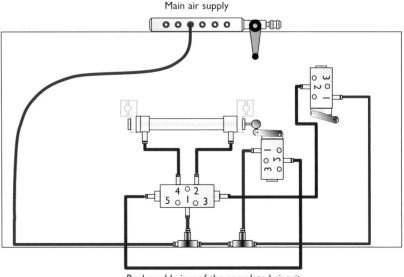

Figure 8.83 *Modelling reciprocating motion*

Real world view of the completed circuit

Hopper system

Design situation

A small biscuit manufacturer wishes to use a hopper system to load a range of their snack bars into a wrapping machine. Design and build a model hopper that will continuously push snack bars into the wrapping machine.

Solution

The solution incorporated reciprocating motion. The push rod had a cam that operated the 3/2 roller trip valves.

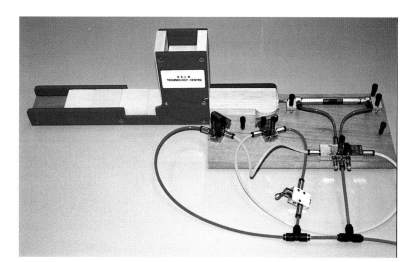

Figure 8.84 *The final solution*

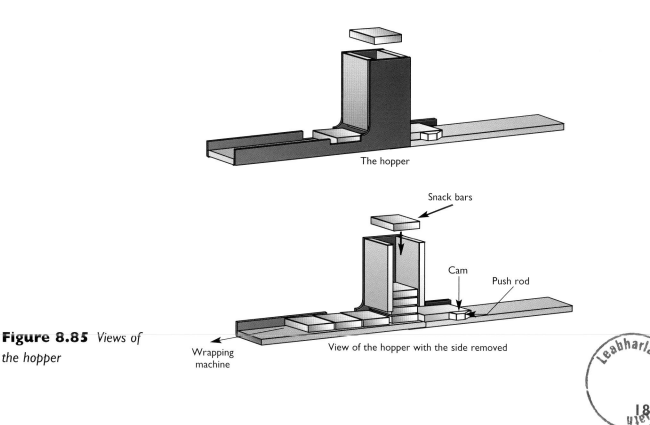

The hopper

Figure 8.85 *Views of the hopper*

Snack bars

Cam

Push rod

Wrapping machine

View of the hopper with the side removed

Modification

During testing it was found that the hopper would become jammed. To enable this to be cleared safely a lever operated 3/2 valve was added to the main air supply going to the roller trip 3/2 valve closest to the cylinder. When the lever operated 3/2 valve was closed, signal air was not able to flow back to the pilot/pilot air operated 5/2 valve with the result the cylinder remained in the negative position.

Index